HMH SCIENCE DIMENSIONS™
Volume 1

Grade 4
Units 1–5

This Write-In Book belongs to

_____

Teacher/Room

_____

Houghton Mifflin Harcourt™

Consulting Authors

Michael A. DiSpezio
Global Educator
North Falmouth, Massachusetts

Marjorie Frank
Science Writer and Content-Area
Reading Specialist
Brooklyn, New York

Michael R. Heithaus, PhD
Dean, College of Arts, Sciences &
Education
Professor, Department of Biological
Sciences
Florida International University
Miami, Florida

Cary Sneider, PhD
Associate Research Professor
Portland State University
Portland, Oregon

Front cover: model car ©GIPhotoStock/Science Source

Back cover: Mars Rover ©NASA/JPL/Cornell University/Maas Digital

Printed in the U.S.A.

ISBN 978-1-328-90512-3

9 10 0868 25 24 23 22 21

4500825226   D E F G

Program Advisors

Paul D. Asimow, PhD
Eleanor and John R. McMillan Professor of Geology and Geochemistry
California Institute of Technology
Pasadena, California

Eileen Cashman, PhD
Professor
Humboldt State University
Arcata, California

Mark B. Moldwin, PhD
Professor of Space Sciences and Engineering
University of Michigan
Ann Arbor, Michigan

Kelly Y. Neiles, PhD
Assistant Professor of Chemistry
St. Mary's College of Maryland
St. Mary's City, Maryland

Sten Odenwald, PhD
Astronomer
NASA Goddard Spaceflight Center
Greenbelt, Maryland

Bruce W. Schafer
Director of K–12 STEM Collaborations, retired
Oregon University System
Portland, Oregon

Barry A. Van Deman
President and CEO
Museum of Life and Science
Durham, North Carolina

Kim Withers, PhD
Assistant Professor
Texas A&M University-Corpus Christi
Corpus Christi, Texas

Adam D. Woods, PhD
Professor
California State University, Fullerton
Fullerton, California

Classroom Reviewers

Michelle Barnett
Lichen K–8 School
Citrus Heights, California

Brandi Bazarnik
Skycrest Elementary
Citrus Heights, California

Kristin Wojes-Broetzmann
Saint Anthony Parish School
Menomonee Falls, Wisconsin

Andrea Brown
District Science and STEAM Curriculum TOSA
Hacienda La Puente Unified School District
Hacienda Heights, California

Denice Gayner
Earl LeGette Elementary
Fair Oaks, California

Emily Giles
Elementary Curriculum Consultant
Kenton County School District
Ft. Wright, Kentucky

Crystal Hintzman
Director of Curriculum, Instruction and Assessment
School District of Superior
Superior, Wisconsin

Roya Hosseini
Junction Avenue K–8 School
Livermore, California

Cynthia Alexander Kirk
Classroom Teacher, Learning Specialist
West Creek Academy
Valencia, California

Marie LaCross
Fair Oaks Ranch Community School
Santa Clarita, California

Emily Miller
Science Specialist
Madison Metropolitan School District
Madison, Wisconsin

Monica Murray, EdD
Principal
Bassett Unified School District
La Puente, California

Wendy Savaske
Director of Instructional Services
School District of Holmen
Holmen, Wisconsin

Tina Topoleski
District Science Supervisor
Jackson School District
Jackson, New Jersey

You are a scientist!

You are naturally curious.

Have you wondered . . .

- is ice still water?
- if you could float in midair?
- how you can talk to your friend on a cell phone?
- if plants can grow without soil?

_____

_____

_____

_____

Write in some other things you wonder about.

HMH SCIENCE DIMENSIONS™

will **SPARK** your curiosity

AND prepare you for

✓ tomorrow
✓ next year
✓ college
or career
✓ life

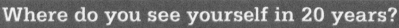

Where do you see yourself in 20 years?

Write in or draw another career you'd like.

Be a scientist.

Work like real scientists work.

Plan

Investigate

Have Fun

Be an engineer.

Solve problems like engineers do.

Design

Solve Problems

Share Solutions

Explain your world.

Start by asking questions.

Think Critically

Make a Claim

Gather Evidence

There's more than one way to the answer. What's YOURS?

Work in Teams

Develop Explanations

Support Your Conclusions

Engineering and Technology

© Houghton Mifflin Harcourt • Image Credits: © Fstop/Alamy Images

Energy

© Houghton Mifflin Harcourt • Image Credits: ©NASA

xii

© Houghton Mifflin Harcourt • Image Credits: ©Allstarecho/Wikimedia Commons

Changes to Earth's Surface ... 349

UNIT 7

Rocks and Fossils 453

© Houghton Mifflin Harcourt • Image Credits: ©alacatr/istock / getty Images Plus/Getty Images

Safety in the Lab

Doing science is a lot of fun. But, a science lab can be a dangerous place. Falls, cuts, and burns can happen easily. **Know the safety rules and listen to your teacher.**

☐ **Think ahead.** Study the investigation steps so you know what to expect. If you have any questions, ask your teacher. Be sure you understand all caution statements and safety reminders.

☐ **Be neat and clean.** Keep your work area clean. If you have long hair, pull it back so it doesn't get in the way. Roll or push up long sleeves to keep them away from your activity.

☐ **Oops!** If you spill or break something, or get cut, tell your teacher right away.

☐ **Watch your eyes.** Wear safety goggles anytime you are directed to do so. If you get anything in your eyes, tell your teacher right away.

☐ **Yuck!** Never eat or drink anything during a science activity.

☐ **Don't get shocked.** Be careful if an electric appliance is used. Be sure that electric cords are in a safe place where you can't trip over them. Never use the cord to pull a plug from an outlet.

☐ **Keep it clean.** Always clean up when you have finished. Put everything away and wipe your work area. Wash your hands.

☐ **Play it safe.** Always know where to find safety equipment, such as fire extinguishers. Know how to use the safety equipment around you.

Safety in the Field

Lots of science research happens outdoors. It's fun to explore the wild! But, you need to be careful. The weather, the land, and the living things can surprise you.

- [ ] **Think ahead.** Study the investigation steps so you know what to expect. If you have any questions, ask your teacher. Be sure you understand all caution statements and safety reminders.

- [ ] **Dress right.** Wear appropriate clothes and shoes for the outdoors. Cover up and wear sunscreen and sunglasses for sun safety.

- [ ] **Clean up the area.** Follow your teacher's instructions for when and how to throw away waste.

- [ ] **Oops!** Tell your teacher right away if you break something or get hurt.

- [ ] **Watch your eyes.** Wear safety goggles when directed to do so. If you get anything in your eyes, tell your teacher right away.

- [ ] **Yuck!** Never taste anything outdoors.

- [ ] **Stay with your group.** Work in the area as directed by your teacher. Stay on marked trails.

- [ ] **"Wilderness" doesn't mean go wild.** Never engage in horseplay, games, or pranks.

- [ ] **Always walk.** No running!

- [ ] **Play it safe.** Know where safety equipment can be found and how to use it. Know how to get help.

- [ ] **Clean up.** Wash your hands with soap and water when you come back indoors.

© Houghton Mifflin Harcourt

Safety Symbols

To highlight important safety concerns, the following symbols are used in a Hands-On Activity. Remember that no matter what safety symbols you see, all safety rules should be followed at all times.

Dress Code

- Wear safety goggles as directed.
- If anything gets into your eye, tell your teacher immediately
- Do not wear contact lenses in the lab.
- Wear appropriate protective gloves as directed.
- Tie back long hair, secure loose clothing, and remove loose jewelry.

Glassware and Sharp Object Safety

- Do not use chipped or cracked glassware.
- Notify your teacher immediately if a piece of glass breaks.
- Use extreme care when handling all sharp and pointed instruments.
- Do not cut an object while holding the object in your hands.
- Cut objects on a suitable surface, always in a direction away from your body.

Electrical Safety

- Do not use equipment with frayed electrical cords or loose plugs.
- Do not use electrical equipment near water or when clothing or hands are wet.
- Hold the plug when you plug in or unplug equipment.

Chemical Safety

- If a chemical gets on your skin, on your clothing, or in your eyes, rinse it immediately, and tell your teacher.
- Do not clean up spilled chemicals unless your teacher directs you to do so.
- Keep your hands away from your face while you are working on any activity.

Heating and Fire Safety

- Know your school's evacuation-fire routes.
- Never leave a hot plate unattended while it is turned on or while it is cooling.
- Allow equipment to cool before storing it.

Plant and Animal Safety

- Do not eat any part of a plant.
- Do not pick any wild plant unless your teacher instructs you to do so.
- Treat animals carefully and respectfully.
- Wash your hands throughly after handling any plant or animal.

Cleanup

- Clean all work surfaces and protective equipment as directed by your teacher.
- Wash your hands throughly before you leave the lab or after any activity.

Safety Quiz

Circle the letter of the BEST answer.

1. Before starting an activity, you should
   a. try an experiment of your own.
   b. open all containers and packages.
   c. read all directions and make sure you understand them.
   d. handle all the equipment to become familiar with it.

2. At the end of any activity you should
   a. wash your hands thoroughly before leaving the lab.
   b. cover your face with your hands.
   c. put on your safety goggles.
   d. leave the materials where they are.

3. If you get hurt or injured in any way, you should
   a. tell your teacher immediately.
   b. find bandages or a first aid kit.
   c. go to your principal's office.
   d. get help after you finish the activity.

4. If your equipment is chipped or broken, you should
   a. use it only for solid materials.
   b. give it to your teacher for recycling or disposal.
   c. put it back.
   d. increase the damage so that it is obvious.

5. If you have unused liquids after finishing an activity, you should
   a. pour them down a sink or drain.
   b. mix them all together in a bucket.
   c. put them back into their original containers.
   d. dispose of them as directed by your teacher.

6. When working with materials that might fly into the air and hurt someone's eye, you should wear
   a. goggles.
   b. an apron.
   c. gloves.
   d. a hat.

7. If you get something in your eye you should
   a. wash your hands immediately.
   b. put the lid back on the container.
   c. wait to see if your eye becomes irritated.
   d. tell your teacher right away.

Engineering and Technology

 Explore Online

Unit Project: Extend a Sense
How can you extend your sense of sight, smell, or touch? You will conduct an investigation with your team. Ask your teacher for details.

When a new rocket is designed, it must be tested.

At a Glance

Vocabulary Game: **Guess the Word**

Materials
• Kitchen timer or online computer timer

Directions

1. Take turns to play.

2. To take a turn, choose a vocabulary word. Do not tell the word to the other players.

3. Set the timer for one minute.

4. Give a one-word clue about your word. Point to a player. That player has one chance to guess your word.

5. Repeat step 4 with other players until a player guesses the word or time runs out. Give a different one-word clue each time.

6. The first player to guess the word gets 1 point. If the player can then use the word in a sentence, he or she gets 1 more point. Then that player chooses the next word.

7. The first player to score 5 points wins.

criteria
The desirable features of a solution.

optimize
To make a solution as good as possible.

Unit Vocabulary

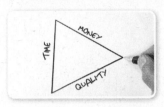

constraint: A real world limit on a solution, for example, safety needs, time, money, or materials.

criteria: The desirable features of a solution.

engineering: The process of designing new or improved techology.

failure analysis: Figuring out what went wrong with a solution and why.

fair test: A test that does not give any advantage to the conditions or objects being tested.

optimize: To make a solution as good as possible.

How Do Engineers Define Problems?

Animals that live in the wild have to catch their own food if they want to eat. A hunter often can hear the prey. The prey often can hear the hunter coming. Think about the ways in which these animals hear the world around them.

By the end of this lesson . . .
you'll be able to define a design problem and identify the constraints and criteria for a design solution.

Can You Solve It?

What sounds do you think the vole makes that the owl could hear? What helps the animals on these two pages find food and protect themselves from being eaten?

1. Think of the sounds living things including birds make. Imagine that your class is going on a nature hike to observe and identify these sounds. As part of your nature hike, you need to design a lightweight hearing-enhancing device that you can wear. It can't use batteries. How would you define this problem?

_____

_____

_____

_____

_____

_____

_____

EVIDENCE NOTEBOOK Look for this icon to help you gather evidence to answer the questions above.

What Is Technology?

What Do You See?

The hearing device problem may seem too hard at first. It's easier if you tackle it in an organized way. First, though, you need to learn a little about technology. Technology is how humans change the natural world to meet a want or a need. **Engineering** is the process of designing new or improved technology. Engineers are the people who do engineering.

The first part of designing a solution is describing what the solution must do. How will it meet a want or need? Examining familiar technology can help you learn to do that.

Kitchen Tech

2. Think about how each technology you see meets a want or need. How did engineers play a role in the technology shown in the picture?

© Houghton Mifflin Harcourt

Engineered?

3. In the first column, write the name of five nonliving things you see in your classroom that are engineered. In the other column, write the name of five nonliving things you see in your classroom that are not engineered. Turn to a partner, and justify your choices for each column.

Engineered	Not engineered

Match the engineering contributions with the technology in the picture.

a. designed tools to melt and form glass; made a process to cut glass and assemble a frame

b. designed tools to cut, fold, and glue sheets of cardboard into containers

c. designed electric circuits, mechanical parts, and an easy-to-use control panel

4. Look at the kitchen scene again, and identify three more examples of technology and the problems they solve. How do you know that these are examples of technology?

_____

_____

_____

_____

_____

_____

_____

_____

_____

_____

What Is the Problem?

View the image of the kitchen again. After you have thought about the specific parts of technology in the kitchen, pick three items in the kitchen that you think best meet a want or need.

5. Write the name of each item in the left-hand column. Write out the need or want that is met by the item in the right-hand column.

Technology item	Need or want met
1.	
2.	
3.	

You have learned that when a need or want is met, engineers have worked to meet the criteria. **Criteria** are desirable features of the solution. For example, you want rags that can soak up liquids. Paper towels were an improvement on rags. Paper towels meet a new criterion—they are made to be thrown away. They still soak up liquids.

A paper towel is designed to be absorbent and strong so it can soak up liquids without ripping.

 EVIDENCE NOTEBOOK What are the criteria for your hearing enhancer?

 Language SmArts
Cite Evidence for Criteria

6. Pick an everyday object, such as a backpack or lunchbox, that you would like to improve. Give the criteria for a successful improvement.

_____

_____

_____

_____

Tip

The English Language Arts Handbook can provide help with understanding how to cite evidence to explain your ideas.

Menu Planning

Objective

Collaborate Engineering solutions can be a plan or process, too. Suppose that you need to plan three main dishes for dinner on three different nights, nine meals all together. Each night, you must analyze your meal options in order to meet a constraint. A **constraint** is a limit on possible solutions. On the first night, you have a constraint that the budget is $35.00.

For each night, choose a main dish from the recipe cards. The constraints for each set of meals are listed in the steps below. Your goal is a set of three main dishes that meet all the constraints.

When you are faced with a problem or situation that needs a solution, how can thinking carefully about the criteria and constraints help you develop one?

Materials
• recipe cards

Procedure

STEP 1 Think of what you would consider a good meal. It may be that the meal is healthy for you, contains well-balanced ingredients, or looks and smells tasty. Write down three criteria for what makes a good meal.

Criteria

1.	
2.	
3.	

STEP 2 Plan out the first set of meals. Choose from the list of recipe cards that meet the constraint of a budget of $35.00. Enter the recipes and costs in the table below. Don't forget to check your math.

	Recipe card	Cost
Meal 1		
Meal 2		
Meal 3		
Total cost		

STEP 3 Now apply the three criteria you picked to the three meals you have put together. Evaluate the quality of the meals using the three criteria. Enter your evaluation below.

_____

_____

STEP 4 Now plan out a second set of meals for the next three nights, choosing from all 12 recipe cards. For this set of meals, your constraints are that you have a budget of $35.00 and a total of 100 minutes to prepare all three meals. The meals must be prepared one at a time. Enter the recipes, costs, and times in the table below.

	Recipe card	Cost	Prep time
Meal 1			
Meal 2			
Meal 3			
Total cost			
Time to prepare all three meals			

STEP 5 Now apply the three criteria you picked before to the three meals you have put together. Evaluate the quality of the meals using the three criteria. Write your evaluation below.

_____

_____

STEP 6 Last, plan out a third set of meals for the last three nights using all 12 recipe cards. Your constraints for this meal are that you have a budget of $35.00, you have a total of 100 minutes to prepare all three meals, and some of your guests are vegetarians. Enter your recipes and the constraints below.

	Recipe card	Cost	Prep time	Vegetarian option
Meal 1				
Meal 2				
Meal 3				
Total Cost				
Time to prepare all three meals				
Number of meal options for vegetarian guests				

STEP 7 Now apply the three criteria you picked before to the three meals you have put together. Evaluate the quality of the meals using the three criteria. Enter your evaluation below.

_____

_____

Analyze Your Results

STEP 8 Which constraint was easiest to plan around? Which constraint was hardest? In both cases, tell how you might have planned differently. Enter your answers in the table below.

Best	
Worst	

Draw Conclusions

STEP 9 What was the goal of the activity? How did your solution help achieve that goal?

_____

_____

STEP 10 Say that another student wants to complete this activity for the first time. What are two things you would tell this student to guide him or her during the activity?

_____

_____

STEP 11 Change one of your criteria. How would this change your recipe selections?

_____

_____

Recipe Cards

1 Chicken and Spinach with Penne Pasta
Cost: $15   **Prep Time:** 30 minutes
Ingredients:
• boneless chicken   • butter
• spinach   • olive oil
• penne pasta

2 Cheeseburgers with French Fries
Cost: $11   **Prep Time:** 40 minutes
Ingredients:
• American sliced cheese   • ground beef
• buns   • french fries

3 Chicken Noodle Soup with a Grilled Cheese Sandwich

Cost: $13   **Prep Time:** 25 minutes

Ingredients:
- canned chicken noodle soup
- sandwich bread
- sliced cheese
- butter

8 Tomato Soup with Grilled Cheese (Vegetarian Option)

Cost: $10   **Prep Time:** 25 minutes

Ingredients:
- canned tomato and basil soup
- sliced sandwich bread
- sliced cheese, butter

4 Shrimp with Rice, Tomatoes, and Olives

Cost: $17   **Prep Time:** 35 minutes

Ingredients:
- large Gulf shrimp
- wild rice
- cherry tomatoes
- black and green olives

9 Vegetable Pizza (Vegetarian Option)

Cost: $14   **Prep Time:** 35 minutes

Ingredients:
- pizza dough
- olive oil
- squash
- goat cheese
- tomato sauce
- green onions
- red peppers

5 Steak with Mixed Vegetables

Cost: $15   **Prep Time:** 30 minutes

Ingredients:
- 8 oz. sirloin steak
- mixed vegetables

10 Tofu Cheeseburgers with French Fries (Vegetarian Option)

Cost: $13   **Prep Time:** 40 minutes

Ingredients:
- tofu mix
- buns
- sliced cheese
- french fries

6 Chicken with Broccoli

Cost: $14   **Prep Time:** 30 minutes

Ingredients:
- 8 oz. chicken breast
- broccoli

11 Beans and Cheese Quesadillas (Vegetarian Option)

Cost: $12   **Prep Time:** 25 minutes

Ingredients:
- black or pinto beans
- shredded cheese
- small tortillas

7 Salmon and Rice

Cost: $17   **Prep Time:** 40 minutes

Ingredients:
- 8 oz. salmon
- brown rice
- olive oil, basil

12 Spaghetti and Marinara Sauce (Vegetarian Option)

Cost: $13   **Prep Time:** 25 minutes

Ingredients:
- marinara sauce
- spaghetti pasta

Real-World Limits

Limited Limits

Part of defining engineering problems is identifying the constraints. A constraint is a limit on possible solutions. Examples of constraints include money, time, and materials. Some safety constraints are required by law.

Bike Tech

7. Match the safety constraints described to the bike parts.

 Explore Online

Paper Building 10 • 10 • 10

8. You have 10 index cards and 10 cm of tape. In 10 minutes, work as a team to build the tallest stucture you can. It should support at least one book. In the space below, list the constraints and tell which was the hardest to meet and why.

_____

_____

_____

a. It helps control speed. Safety regulations say that a 68 kg (150 lb) bicycle rider moving at 24 km/hr (15 mph) must be able to use them to stop within 4.5 m (15 ft).

b. It undergoes great force as you pedal. Grit from the road causes wear, and water rusts it. Safety regulations say it must withstand a pull of 818 kg (1,800 lb) before breaking.

c. This part supports your weight while you ride. Its height is adjustable. Safety regulations say it must support a weight of 68 kg (150 lb) without moving down.

9. Describe another possible constraint for a bicycle. Look back at the bicycle image for different ideas. Enter your answer below.

_____

_____

_____

_____

_____

_____

_____

_____

_____

_____

_____

_____

Improvements

Engineers improve solutions all the time. A new solution may not work for everyone, though. Some people may have constraints, such as money or available space, on the solutions they can decide to buy or use.

laundry basket

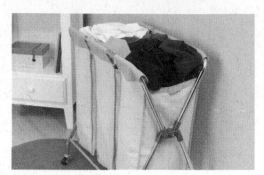

three-bin laundry basket

10. Look at the laundry baskets. How is the three-bin basket an improvement? What contraints might a buyer have that would keep them from using the improved solution?

_____

_____

_____

 EVIDENCE NOTEBOOK Think back to your hearing enhancer. What constraints are there on your solution?

11. Remember, criteria are features of a desirable solution, while constraints are limits that must be met in order to be acceptable. In the following lists of criteria and constraints, draw a star next to each constraint.

A new pair of shoes	A homework assignment
comfortable	neatly written
resists water	shows originality
attractive	completed by tomorrow's class
costs less than $35	good grammar

Discover More

Check out this path . . . or go online to choose one of these other paths.

People in
Science

• Writing within Constraints
• Limits in Nature

Marion Downs

Marion Downs was an audiologist, a doctor specializing in hearing. She helped many thousands of children to speak and hear better by noticing and solving a problem.

Infants born with hearing problems can't hear their own voice or the voices of others. So, they can't develop language skills. Infants can't talk at first, anyway. So, before the 1960s, it took two or three years to notice an infant's hearing problem.

Dr. Downs engineered a hearing test that didn't require infants to talk. Instead, a doctor watched them respond to sounds, such as a rattles. A second part of the solution was to change what doctors do nationwide. Now, doctors screen all six-month-old infants to see if they might need hearing aids.

One type of hearing aid infants receive is a cochlear implant. This hearing aid is implanted under the skin, behind the ear. It converts sounds to electrical signals that are sent to the inner ear.

Although Dr. Downs was not an engineer, she engineered a solution to a serious gap in our nation's health system.

Explore
Online

Marion Downs, audiologist

Cochlear implant

Protecting Hearing

Noise is a major cause of hearing loss later in life. The loss can be temporary after being exposed to a loud noise, such as a firecracker. It might take a day or more to recover. A person can have permanent hearing loss if he or she is exposed to loud noises for long periods of time. Loud music, jet engine noise, and gunfire can cause permanent hearing loss.

Musicians, construction workers, or others who have jobs in loud noise environments can protect their sense of hearing from permanent damage. Devices like over-the-ear hearing protectors block loud noises from damaging the sense of hearing.

Dense foam earplugs also protect the ear from loud noises. They are flexible and fit snugly in the ear canal.

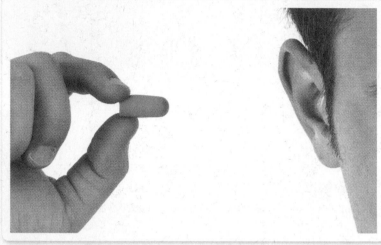

Dense foam earplugs

Over-ear hearing protectors

12. What are some criteria for hearing aids? for hearing protectors? What are some constraints?

_____

_____

_____

_____

_____

_____

13. Research how people have their hearing tested. Summarize what you find below. Include an idea that you want to explore more. Be prepared to share your findings.

_____

_____

_____

Lesson Check

Name _____

Can You Solve It?

1. In the next lesson, you will develop a device to enhance your ability to hear sounds in the wild.

    • What does your hearing enhancer need to do? What are the limits on its design?

    • Make sure to use the words *criteria* and *constraints*.

    _____

    _____

 EVIDENCE NOTEBOOK Use the information you've collected in your Evidence Notebook to help you cover each point above.

_____

_____

_____

_____

_____

_____

_____

Checkpoints

Answer the questions that follow about how engineers define problems.

2. Choose all the statements that are correct.

    a. Solutions meet a want or need.

    b. Solutions are separate from engineering.

    c. Solutions are the technology all around us.

    d. Solutions come in different forms because they help solve problems.

    e. Solutions must be complicated in order to work.

3. Which statement is true of solutions?

   a. Solutions do not meet a want or need.

   b. Solutions can be tested.

   c. Solutions are the limitations of a problem.

   d. Solutions are the technology of a problem.

4. Janet is trying to improve the design of her lunchbox. Choose all of following statements that are good criteria for her to keep in mind.

   a. The lunchbox can't be too heavy to hold for a long time.

   b. The lunchbox should have sharp corners and rough edges.

   c. The lunchbox could use a special pocket for water bottles.

   d. The lunchbox could keep food colder.

5. Identify all the likely constraints faced when designing and building a two-room treehouse.

   a. time   **d.** sunlight

   b. budget   **e.** tree size

   c. materials   **f.** number of rooms

6. Choose the correct word to complete the sentence.

   In a room full of objects, we can think of different technology objects

   as _____ because they help satisfy a want or need.

   | criteria |
   | solutions |
   | constraints |
   | problems |

7. Draw lines to match each word to its description.

engineering		desired features of a solution
constraints		identification of a want or need
criteria		using technology to design solutions to solve problems
problem		absolute limits on a solution

8. Write the name of the item from the picture that uses technology to fill each need or want.

   a. keep warm _____

   b. protect the head _____

   c. improve vision _____

   d. adjust speed and force _____

20

Lesson Roundup

A. Choose the best words from the word bank to complete the sentences.

a specific weight	limitations	requirements
criteria	solutions	

Good criteria tell _____ an engineering solution should meet.

Constraints are the _____ on an engineering solution.

B. Choose the best words from the word bank to complete the sentences.

solutions	criteria	constraints	weather and day of the week
a budget and a time limit	brand of bike and criteria		

Omar is going to try to improve his bicycle. He first looks to see what his

limitations, or _____, are. He knows that the biggest limit is

how much money he can spend. He also must have the bike ready to ride in a race

in two weeks. His constraints are _____.

C. Choose the best words from the word bank to complete the sentences.

solutions	other materials	books	design
solution	requirements	limitations	criteria

Engineering _____ have different criteria and constraints.

These criteria describe _____. The constraints describe the

_____ for the engineering solution.

How Do Engineers Design Solutions?

Think about the bird calls and other sounds you might hear on a nature walk. Observing and identifying those sounds can be a challenge.

By the end of this lesson . . .
you'll research and design possible solutions to a problem and investigate how well your solution performs.

Can You Solve It?

Recall the nature hike scenario that you read about in the last lesson. You thought about the criteria and constraints for a hearing-enhancing device. This device would help you and others better hear the wildlife on your walk.

1. What might your hearing-enhancing device look like? Why? How will the constraints and criteria affect its appearance? Enter your answers below.

_____

_____

_____

_____

_____

_____

_____

_____

_____

Tip

For more information about what engineers do, review How Do Engineers Define Problems?

 EVIDENCE NOTEBOOK Look for this icon to help you gather evidence to answer the questions above.

Research Matters!

Ears to You!

Designing a solution can be tough. Depending on the situation, there can be many different steps. One important first step is to learn more about the problem before you start to design a solution.

Your challenge is to design a hearing-enhancing device to use on a nature walk. Where should you start? You might want to start by learning how different animals use hearing to solve their problems. View each image below, and read the captions to explore how some animals use hearing to solve different problems.

The fox is an excellent hunter. It uses its hearing to locate small mammals that burrow underground. When the fox figures out where an animal is, it will dig it up.

Mule deer are common in the western United States. These animals have large ears that allow them to hear sounds, such as those made by predators which can pose dangers.

Aye-ayes live on Madagascar. They tap on tree bark with their long fingers and use their ears to listen for moving larvas. When they hear the larvas, they use their fingers to pry them out of the bark and eat them.

Wild rabbits live in many temperate environments. These animals can independently rotate their ears to pick up the softest of sounds. Rabbits use their hearing to identify possible predators.

Look again at the photos on the previous page and recall what you read. Use this information to complete the table below. Then answer the question to explain how animals can use hearing to solve problems.

Ears, Ears, Ears

2. In the table, make a detailed drawing of each animal's ear.

Type of animal	Shape of ear
Red fox	
Mule deer	
Aye-aye	
Wild rabbit	

3. How do the ears of these animals differ? How are they the same? How can looking at these animals' ears help you design your hearing-enhancing device?

_____

_____

_____

_____

Targeting Sounds

As you have just learned, hearing is an important sense for many animals. It helps them to survive in their environments. It helps them find food and avoid predators or other dangers. View the photos on these pages and think about the sounds each songbird makes. How could your hearing enhancer help you hear differences between the songs?

Explore Online

North American Songbirds

The black-capped chickadee is a songbird often found near wooded areas. Its most often heard song is short whistled two or three note 'fee-bee" or "fee-bee-bee."

The American robin is a common songbird. It often sings just before daylight. Some describe its song as "cheerily cheer-up cheer-up cheerily cheer-up."

The northern cardinal is often found near dense, bushy areas. Its song can be described as a quick and lively "birdie birdie birdie." It signals danger with a loud, short "chip."

The yellow warbler lives in dense woody areas and swamps. Its song sounds like, "sweet sweet sweet, I'm so sweet."

 EVIDENCE NOTEBOOK Apply what you read on this page to possible features of your hearing-enhancing device.

Wildlife, including songbirds, use sounds to communicate and survive in their environments. Think about the similarities and differences between the songs of the North American songbirds that you just read about, and answer the question below.

 Language SmArts
Comparing and Contrasting

4. What is the same about the birds' songs? What is different? What else might you need to help you determine what type of bird you are listening to?

_____

_____

_____

_____

_____

_____

Tip

The English Language Arts Handbook can provide help with understanding how to compare and contrast.

Past Hearing Helpers

Looking Back to Look Forward

Solutions to problems can have many different parts. Looking at others' solutions can often help improve an existing design. In other words, we can learn from past solutions to help us with new and better solutions.

Many hearing-enhancing devices have been made over time. Most are not perfect solutions, though. Engineers continue to build on and work to improve solutions like these hearing aids from the past and present.

This early ear trumpet collected and directed sound waves to the listener's ear. The device worked best when the sounds were nearby. The small end is held near the ear.

Ear trumpets with longer tubes helped amplify sounds, too. They were easier to hold and direct toward the sound.

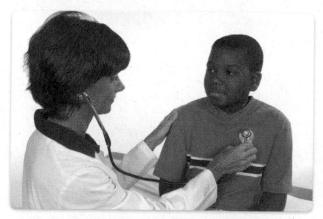

A stethoscope is often used in medicine. Sound travels from the person to the cup, which increases the volume of the sound. The sound moves through the tubes to the user's ears.

This concrete listening post collects and focuses sounds like a curved mirror. Before radar, it was used to listen for approaching enemy planes.

5. Look again at the photos on the previous page. In the table below, describe each device in your own words. Then tell how you think you could change the device to improve it.

Description	How I might improve device
Ear trumpet	
Ear trumpet with a long tube	
Stethoscope	
British acoustic mirror listening post	

6. How might you use what you've learned here to design your hearing-enhancing device?

_____

_____

_____

_____

_____

_____

Hear Here

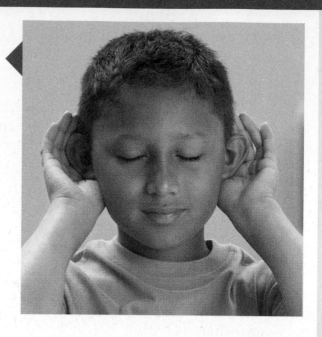

7. Work with a partner. Stand about 3 meters apart. Turn so that your ear is pointing toward your partner. Close your eyes. Have your partner whisper your name. Have your partner whisper your name again, but cup your hands to your ears. Compare the two sounds. Trade roles with your partner so that he or she can observe your whispering. Describe the sounds below. Why did they sound different? Can cupping your hands to your ears make it easier to locate a faint sound? Test and see.

_____

_____

_____

_____

_____

_____

 EVIDENCE NOTEBOOK How can your results from this activity help you design your device?

Putting It Together

8. How does studying others' hearing-enhancing solutions help you with your possible design? How does looking at different types of animals' ears help you with your design?

_____

_____

_____

_____

Passing the Test

Testing, Testing, 1, 2, 3

Engineers design many things that people depend on. It's not enough for an engineer to say that a design works. It needs to be tested to ensure it solves the problem. Each design starts out as a prototype, or early version for testing. Prototypes must be thoroughly tested to be sure they're safe and work correctly. Often, it takes many prototypes to get one that is ideal. Most types of engineering solutions are like this. They need to be tested and improved many times before they meet criteria and satisfy contraints of safety, time, money, or materials.

Anechoic means "no echoes." An *anechoic chamber* is used to test speakers, headphones, and microphones. The walls in the chamber are designed to absorb sound waves.

More Testing

Look at photos below. Then read the captions to learn more about some other engineering designs and how they are tested.

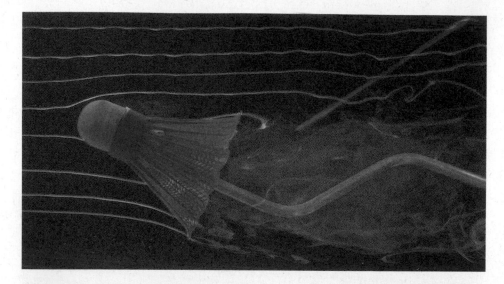

An *aquadynamic* testing facility is similar to a wind tunnel. It is used to test vehicles and objects that move through water to make sure they are safe and do not leak. It is also used to model movement through air.

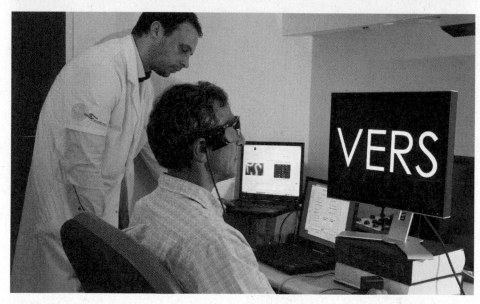

This is an eye-tracking rig. It keeps a record of eye movements while a person uses software or a web page. Portable, wearable devices are used in sports to see if players are really keeping their eyes on the ball!

9. Choose the word or words that correctly complete each sentence.

anechoic chamber	**eye-tracking rig**	**final design**
improve	**prototype**	

A _____ is an early version of a design solution. These versions are tested to help _____ a design solution. An _____ might be tested by a rock band to help with their recordings. Video gamers might use an _____ to test and improve their gaming skills.

Fair Tests

Testing and retesting solutions is important. A **fair test** is one that doesn't give any advantage to the conditions or objects being tested. For a fair test, engineers observe and measure the effects of changing only one thing, or *variable*, at a time. Changing many variables at once seems faster. However, you don't know what causes the results.

Here's an example of a fair test. Suppose you want to find the fastest way to walk home. You'd need to time each route walking at roughly the same speed on similar days. You would not compare walking the first route, running the second, and carrying a heavy backpack on the third. The same is true for the results on a slippery, icy day and on a warm, dry day.

Learn More About Sound Tests

Look at the sound system test room below. You may have seen one like it in a store. Read each caption to find out more about different parts. Then answer the question on the next page.

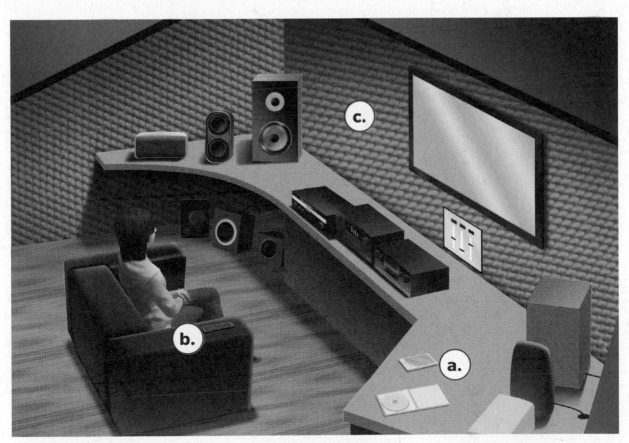

a. Sound source
A CD, smartphone, TV, or radio is a possible source of test sounds.

b. Remote control
A remote control adjusts loudness and chooses the speakers being tested.

c. Wall lining
The wall lining helps keep outside sounds from interfering with the music.

Your Fair Test

10. What steps would you take to make a fair test of a the speakers shown in the sound system test room?

_____

_____

_____

_____

_____

_____

 EVIDENCE NOTEBOOK Explain how the criteria for your hearing-enhancing device affect what you will test.

Putting It Together

11. What factors will your team need to think about and address in order to make a fair test of your hearing-enhancing device?

_____

_____

_____

_____

_____

_____

_____

_____

_____

_____

HANDS-ON ACTIVITY
Design It!

Objective

Collaborate with a team to design your own hearing-enhancing device. Make sure you use the design criteria and constraints as you construct your device. Also use what you've learned about past solutions, animals' ears, and fair tests. Be safe—don't put *anything* in your ears.

What problem will you solve to meet this objective?

_____

_____

_____

Possible Materials

- plastic cups
- paper cups
- cloth scraps
- duct tape
- masking tape
- wire clothes hangers
- string
- rubber tubing
- plastic head bands
- scissors
- baseball or painter's cap

Procedure

STEP 1 Handle and examine the materials available to you. Brainstorm ideas with your team. Choose the best one. Then, make a rough sketch in the box of how you think your device will look and work.

What is the constraint? _____

What are your criteria? _____

_____

STEP 2 Identify the materials from those available that you will use to make your design come to life. Write your list in the first box below. Also write how the materials will help to meet the criteria.

First Design Notes

STEP 3 With your team, build and test your device. Use the test results to improve the device. Stop testing and improving when you are satisfied that it meets the constraints and criteria. In the space below, keep a record of the design changes you make. Include a reason for each change.

Additional Design Notes

STEP 4 When you are satisfied that it meets the constraints and criteria, think of a different design that might work even better. If there is time, build and text a second device that is different in some way.

STEP 5 Use the final design and your notes to answer the questions in the table below.

a. Why did you choose each material? How did they help your design?	
b. Why did you pick this design?	
c. How well did your design meet the criteria and constraints? Explain.	

Analyze Your Results

STEP 6 Did your design meet the goals of this activity? Support your claim with evidence and reasoning.

_____

_____

STEP 7 Explain why you chose two of your materials.

_____

_____

Draw Conclusions

STEP 8 If other students looked at your final design, what improvements did they suggest? Why?

_____

_____

Discover More

Check out this path . . . or go online to choose one of these other paths.

Careers in Science & Engineering

- **Hearing Aid History**
- **Don't Make a Move . . .**

Acoustic Engineer

Engineers work in many fields. An acoustic engineer solves problems related to sound or hearing. From concert halls to quiet cars, acoustic engineers design sound-related objects and systems. They study engineering, physics, and math to be successful. The tools of their trade are microphones, computers, and their ears.

An acoustic engineer might work with concert hall designers to ensure that the venue will absorb and reflect sounds so that the concertgoers enjoy the performances.

an acoustic test lab

Acoustic engineers can design concert halls so the sounds that come from the stage sound great no matter where you sit. Like all engineers, they make and test multiple solutions until they are the best they can be within the design constraints and criteria.

Direct sound

This shows the paths of sound reflection in an auditorium.

12. Describe two or three problems that an acoustic engineer might help solve.

_____

_____

_____

_____

_____

Make Some Sound Observations

13. Look around the room you are in. List at least three different materials that the room itself and objects within it are made of. Write the materials on the lines in the table. Speak softly with your mouth about three inches away from the material. Listen for differences in the sound of your voice. Record your observations.

Material	Observations

14. Based on your observations of how the materials affected the sound of your voice, which materials would you use in a music hall? Which materials would you avoid? Why?

_____

_____

_____

_____

Do the Math
Measuring Sound

15. Human hearing is amazingly sensitive. We can hear sounds from a pin dropping to a landslide. Sound is measured in decibels (dB). A sound that you can barely hear is 0 dB. A quiet whisper that is 10 times louder is 10 dB. A sound that is 100 times louder is 20 dB. A sound that is 1,000 times louder is 30 dB. Complete the table.

Sound	Decibels	Times Louder
whisper	10 dB	10 times
country sounds	20 dB	100 times
city sounds	30 dB	
big truck	90 dB	
rock band	100 dB	

Lesson Check

Name _____

Can You Solve It?

Explore Online

1. Recall the imaginary nature hike and your proposed solution for a hearing-enhancing device. Use what you've learned to do the following:

   • Explain the importance of researching previous solutions to the same problem.

   • Explain how solutions are designed.

   • Describe how and why potential design solutions are tested.

> **EVIDENCE NOTEBOOK** Use the information you've collected in your Evidence Notebook to help you cover each point above.

_____

_____

_____

_____

_____

_____

_____

_____

Checkpoints

2. Choose the word or words that correctly complete each sentence.

solutions	problems	audio
acoustics	fair tests	old prototypes

Engineers design _____ to help solve problems. They perform

_____ to help them design new devices.

3. Draw lines to sort each of the following descriptions of the engineering design process into the correct category—**Good Design Practice** or **Poor Design Practice**.

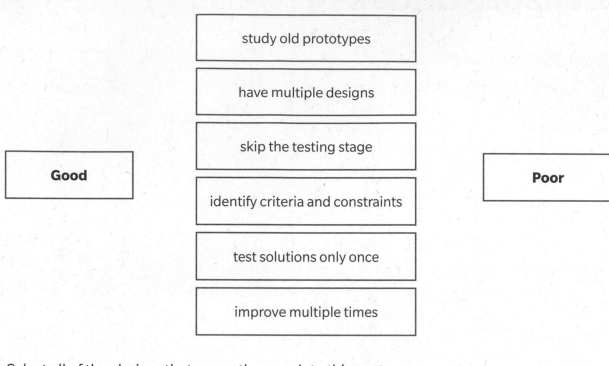

Good

study old prototypes

have multiple designs

skip the testing stage

identify criteria and constraints

test solutions only once

improve multiple times

Poor

4. Select all of the choices that correctly complete this sentence.

Engineers _____
a. test solutions to design problems more than once.
b. don't waste time learning about other solutions to their problems.
c. don't try to improve others' solutions or their own solutions.
d. create more than one solution to the same problem.

5. You've learned that animals use their hearing to solve problems. Which of these problems can they solve using this sense? Select all that apply.
a. finding food
b. swimming faster or slower
c. locating dangerous predators
d. sleeping well at night

6. Choose words from the word bank to complete the sentences.

many tries	retest	retesting
test	testing	one try

Engineers _____ designs because it's important to be

sure a solution works. Usually _____ happens because it takes

_____ to get a working prototype.

Lesson Roundup

A. A new student just joined your class and needs to get caught up on this lesson. What should she do to begin designing her hearing-enhancing device?

    a. research careers in acoustic engineering

    b. study the devices already made by other students

    c. learn how different birds sing different types of songs

    d. ask for materials other than those available

B. Which of these should the new student learn more about at this point? Select all that apply.

    a. ear trumpets

    b. light and mirrors

    c. stethoscopes

    d. sound waves

C. It's your job to tutor the new student so that she quickly catches up. Pretend that you will give her the paragraph below to help her. Choose the words to correctly complete the sentences that she will read.

one part	**many parts**	**no prototype**
multiple prototypes	**test them only once**	**retest them many times**

Like actual engineers, we are solving a problem. Thus, we should create

_____ of our hearing-enhancing devices. Then we should

_____. During our tests, we should change _____

of the design at a time.

D. What do professional engineers do during the design process? Select all that apply.

    a. use prototypes

    b. test each design only once

    c. come up with a single solution

    d. research on existing solutions

    e. change multiple things when testing

    f. meet all of the constraints and as many criteria as possible

How Do Engineers Test and Improve Prototypes?

Crash dummies test what happens to humans in car crashes. Since the 1950s, the dummies have gotten smarter! Some early dummies were much smaller than average humans. Others didn't collect good data. Testing and redesign have made today's crash dummies more effective than those in the past.

By the end of this lesson . . .
you'll collaborate to improve your hearing device and determine a design that best solves the problem.

© Houghton Mifflin Harcourt • Image Credits: ©Fstop/Alamy Images

Can You Solve It?

Early rocket designs often failed with their first tests. They ended with crashes and fiery explosions. Future designs were improved to solve those problems.

1. How can collaboration and communication lead to improving your hearing-enhancing device prototype?

_____

_____

_____

_____

_____

_____

Tip

In this lesson you'll work on the hearing device you've been designing. For more information about what engineers do, review How Do Engineers Define Problems?

EVIDENCE NOTEBOOK Look for this icon to help you gather evidence to answer the question above.

Class Collaboration

Objective

In the past two lessons, you learned how to define engineering problems and design engineering solutions. You have also learned how to apply these skills to designing a hearing-enhancing device. Recall that the purpose of this device is to help someone observe and identify natural sounds during a nature walk.

Collaborate Work with your class to further improve your team's design from the previous lesson. First, collect your team's device or gather the materials you need to rebuild it.

What problem will you solve to meet this objective?

_____

_____

_____

Possible Materials

- safety goggles
- plastic cups
- paper cups
- cloth scraps
- duct tape
- masking tape
- wire clothes hangers
- string
- rubber tubing
- plastic head bands
- scissors
- baseball or painter's cap

Procedure

STEP 1 Recall your design criteria and constraints. List them on the lines below. Rank the criteria in order of importance. Remember them as your class works to improve your designs.

_____

_____

_____

_____

_____

_____

STEP 2 Demonstrate and explain your team's design for your class. Tell which features and materials worked best. As the other teams demonstrate, take notes below. List features that you might use to improve your team's design.

Notes from demonstrations

STEP 3 Choose one feature to improve based on your notes in Step 2. It should support one of your top-ranked criteria. Plan and build your improved device.

STEP 4 As a team, plan a fair test of your improved design. Write down the test procedure you will use in the table below. Test your design. Record your test results. If you need to, keep revising and testing your design until you are satisfied with the improvement.

Test plan and results
Test plan
Test results

Analyze Your Results

STEP 5 What improvement did your team add and why did you choose it?

_____

_____

STEP 6 Did your team's design pass your test? Explain.

_____

_____

STEP 7 If you could add or change another feature to improve your design, what would it be? Why?

_____

_____

Draw Conclusions

STEP 8 State a claim about your improved design and how it tested. Cite evidence from the activity to support your claim.

_____

_____

_____

STEP 9 If you could start over with designing your hearing-enhancing device, how would you do it? Explain.

_____

_____

_____

_____

STEP 10 What questions came to you about the task of designing and testing prototypes?

_____

_____

Things Fail and Improve

Try, Try Again!

You've learned that engineering solutions are designed and built to solve a problem. Often, perhaps like what happened with your hearing-enhancing device, a first design doesn't work. For example, a design might work okay, but testing suggests that it can work a lot better. Or the design might meet almost all of the criteria but be unsafe. When this happens, engineers head back to the drawing board to improve their designs.

Designs can also improve bit by bit as engineers learn more about the materials they're using. Small positive changes build up as engineers test and add them to the design. The end result is the ideal, or best, design possible within the constraints of time, materials, and budget.

 HANDS-ON **Apply What You Know**

Tissue Rope

2. Look at the rope shown here. Suppose you need to make your own, but out of toilet paper.

   - Your goal is to work with a partner to find the best toiletpaper rope-making technique you can. You are limited to 15 minutes to explore and build. A loop of your product will be tested to see how much weight it will support.

   - Get two arm-lengths of toilet paper from your teacher.

   - Wait for your teacher to say "start." Then, with your partner, figure out the best way to turn the paper into a rope.

   - Try lots of ideas! When you are happy with your technique, get more paper from your teacher and make your test sample. Be sure to budget time for this.

Was your final product better or worse than your first attempt? Tell how your rope-making technique changed as you tried different ideas.

_____

_____

_____

Cakes Done Right!

Engineers test their designs many times to get the best solution. Tests help them figure out what went wrong and why. This process is called **failure analysis.** It requires thinking carefully about causes and effects, especially for more complex devices or systems.

3. Review the process of testing your hearing-enhancing device. Use your testing and results to complete a failure analysis on your solution. Use the table below to record your thoughts and ideas.

What didn't work?	Why I think it didn't work	How can I fix or improve it?	How critical it is to fix the solution?

Engineers improve designs by careful testing, one system part at a time. They work this way to zero in on an ideal solution for given criteria—the best bicycle, the clearest window, or even the best tasting cake. Read below about recreating Grandma's famous yellow cake.

Too high, too low, too dry . . . just right!

4. Look at the test bake pictures and the information for each test cake. Then write in the likely ideal recipe choices below.

Grandma's Ideal Cake

You're trying to match this cake's taste and look. Based on the test cakes, what are these recipe details?

Use _____ of baking powder.

Bake for _____ minutes.

- This test cake tastes about right. It has 3 teaspoons of baking powder to make it puff up. It baked for 30 minutes at 350 °F.
- How does it compare to the ideal cake you're trying to match?

- This test cake also tastes okay, although it's a little chewy. It has 1 teaspoon of baking powder and baked for 25 minutes at 350 °F.
- How does it compare to the ideal cake you're trying to match?

- This test cake tastes about right. It's dry and crumbly, though. It baked for 35 minutes at 350 °F. Two teaspoons of baking powder were used to make this cake.
- How does it compare to the ideal cake you're trying to match?

 EVIDENCE NOTEBOOK Summarize your response to item 3 in your Evidence Notebook.

Putting It Together

5. Choose the correct word to complete each sentence.

destroy	failure	imperfect	improve	problem solving	perfect

Most prototypes are _____. When testing a design

solution, it is critical to go through a _____ analysis. This

helps _____ a solution.

Getting Better

Talking to the Team

When engineers work on design solutions, team members often communicate with each other. They share their observations to help improve what they are working on and to perhaps gain insight on future solutions.

Communication is an important part of most situations. Like an engineering team, a volleyball team needs to communicate. By talking or giving each other signals during practice, players work as a team and will likely play better during a game.

▷ **Explore Online**

a. Players communicate what the next play will be. The player who plans to hit the ball first calls, "Got it!"

b. Players signal so everyone knows where the ball is going. The second player is ready and waiting to make the second hit.

© Houghton Mifflin Harcourt • Image Credits: ©JOHN MACDOUGALL/AFP/Getty Images

c. The third player is in motion and ready to return the ball over the net.

After a game, volleyball players may talk about what worked well and what didn't work so well. They also may talk about what they plan on doing better during their next practice or game. Likewise, engineers communicate after testing solutions to try to **optimize,** or make as good as possible, their solutions and designs. Good communication and teamwork help improve any team's final results.

6. How is communication important to both sports and engineering?

_____

_____

_____

_____

_____

7. Which of these do you think are ways to improve communication among team members? Circle all that apply.
   a. Tell a team member that her design is well done, and suggest an improvement.
   b. Tell a team member her project is bad, and she shouldn't even test it.
   c. Give a team member some suggestions for alternative materials.
   d. Yell at a team member until he agrees with your viewpoint.
   e. Talk to others about the way they tested their project, and suggest more good tests.
   f. Tell a team member he used the materials wrong, even though his design tested well.

Sharing Feedback

8. Now that you've learned about the importance of communication, team up with two other students and take turns giving feedback on each of your designs. After you have considered one another's feedback, make a plan to retest and improve your hearing-enhancing device.

9. These steps show a process for designing solutions. Write an *A* by steps you learned about in Lesson 1, a *B* for Lesson 2, and a *C* for Lesson 3.

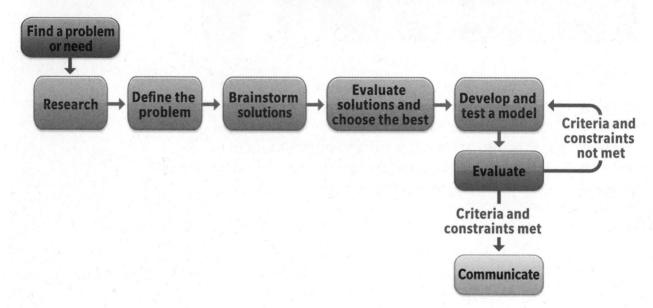

 EVIDENCE NOTEBOOK Use what you've learned in this lesson to describe how you can optimize your solution.

 Language SmArts
Recalling Relevant Information

10. Think about what you learned during the testing of your device. Also think about the feedback you got from others. Use this relevant information to explain what you've learned about the last few steps of an engineering design process.

_____

_____

_____

_____

Tip

The *English Language Arts Handbook* can provide help with understanding how to find and use relevant information to answer questions.

Discover More

Check out this path . . . or go online to choose one of these other paths.

Sense
Extenders
for Science

- **Ear Areas**
- **High or Low?**

Sense Extenders for Science

Scientists and engineers use many different types of tools to extend their senses. Some tools enhance their ability to see objects that are very far away or too small to see with the unaided eye. Other tools amplify sound or allow their users to see what's inside the human body. Some tools produce images that can be studied at a later time.

All of the tools shown on these two pages have been redesigned over time to extend human senses.

The first telescopes were invented in the early 17th century. **Refracting telescopes,** such as this one, use lenses to magnify objects. Over time, these tools were improved to make their lenses larger and clearer.

Hydrophones are underwater microphones. The earliest ones were used in the 1920s by ship captains to communicate. Today, hydrophones have many uses, including listening to whales communicate.

In 1667, Robert Hooke used a simple **light microscope** to observe tiny living things. Today, complex light microscopes are used in many fields of science, including biology and geology.

Thermographic cameras produce images using infrared radiation. Such cameras were first used in the early 1900s to help soldiers see at night. Today, these cameras are used to study rocks that could cause earthquakes, to study galaxies that are far away, to determine if farm animals are sick, to identify dangerous pollutants in the environment, and to inspect buildings and other structures for damage or poor construction.

11. How would you use a thermographic camera?

_____

_____

_____

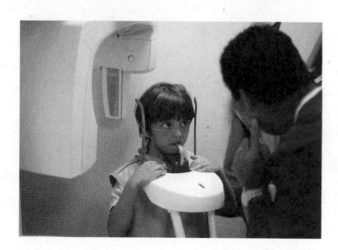

X-rays were discovered in 1895. These rays can pass through skin and tissue but not denser materials, such as teeth and bones. X-rays are used to determine if teeth are healthy, bones are broken, or tumors are present in the body. They can also be used to treat some cancerous tumors.

X-rays are also used at airports to screen for dangerous materials inside suitcases, to learn about the minerals that make up rocks, and even to study objects in space.

12. Research one of the tools on these pages. Or find another tool that extends other senses. Draw the tool and show how it works. Describe how an engineer might use the tool to solve a problem or test a solution.

Lesson Check

Name _____

Can You Solve It?

1. Now that you know about the importance of testing prototypes, apply what you've learned to the rocket example. Be sure to do the following:

- Explain why multiple solutions should be developed and tested.

- Discuss the importance of identifying failure points.

- Describe why communication is critical to any team of people working together.

 EVIDENCE NOTEBOOK Use the information you've collected in your Evidence Notebook to help you cover each point above.

_____
_____
_____
_____
_____
_____
_____

Checkpoints

2. How is communication an important part of designing solutions? Choose all of the statements that are correct.

- **a.** Communication helps people talk about improvement.
- **b.** Communication helps identify problems.
- **c.** Communication only causes arguments.
- **d.** Communication creates a sense of teamwork.
- **e.** Communication is critical only if everyone agrees.

3. Choose the correct words to complete each sentence.

not build	test	throw away
multiple times	once	once and then stop
mistakes	testing	original problem

When building and designing an engineering solution, it is always

important to _____ the solution. Good engineers will

always try to test a solution _____. It is important to keep

in mind the _____ that the solution was meant to solve

when designing and testing a solution.

4. Circle the letter of each correct statement.
   a. Making good observations is important.
   b. Making good observations helps to figure out what needs
      to be improved.
   c. Making good observations shows you what to test next.
   d. Making good observations is not important because it slows
      down the process.
   e. Making good observations can be distracting and should be
      stopped when it happens.

5. An engineer is testing a solution. The solution is failing. What should
   she do? Select all that apply.
   a. She should consider using other materials for the same design.
   b. She should figure out what didn't go right with her design.
   c. She should understand that sometimes things don't work as
      planned.
   d. She should not try to develop other solutions to this problem.

6. Feedback is important in solving any problem. Select the best
   example of how to give good feedback.
   a. Tell the other person that his or her project is a good example of
      what not to do.
   b. Tell the person that his or her design is poorly built. Do not
      suggest any improvements.
   c. Tell the person that his or her design is built well but still suggest
      some possible improvements.
   d. Ignore the person if he or she isn't listening to you.

Lesson Roundup

A. Which of these describes a good approach to solving an engineering problem? Select all that apply.

   a. Research, revise, and repeat.

   b. Give up if your first solution fails so that you don't waste any more of your time.

   c. Failure marks the end of the process.

   d. If at first you don't succeed, try, try again.

B. Explain why an engineering design solution that does not pass testing can be considered a successful solution.

_____

_____

_____

_____

C. Below are steps that you might follow to solve an engineering problem. Add numbers to put them in order.

   a. Test the prototype. _____

   b. Perform failure analysis. _____

   c. Identify criteria and constraints. _____

   d. Test final design. _____

   e. Create the prototype. _____

   f. Identify the problem that needs solving. _____

   g. Choose materials for the prototype. _____

   h. Improve prototype. _____

   i. Research information about the problem. _____

ENGINEER IT!

Designing a Portable Chair

You work for a company that builds seating for large events. Clients are complaining that the portable chairs you make are not comfortable. It is your team's task to learn about portable chairs and design one that your clients will like.

Clients don't like sitting on this.

STATING YOUR GOAL: How will you know that you have completed your assignment?

_____

_____

Review the checklist at the end of this Unit Performance Task. Keep those requirements in mind as you proceed.

RESEARCH: Study the portable chairs that are currently on the market. Find out which are the most popular. Note their features. Examine several online or library resources, and cite them.

_____

_____

_____

BRAINSTORM: Brainstorm three or more ideas with your team that might fit with your goal. Evaluate the ideas, and choose the best based on the criteria of the project.

_____

_____

_____

_____

_____

© Houghton Mifflin Harcourt • Image Credits: ©Artville/Getty Images

MAKE A PLAN: Plan a design for your chair by considering the questions below.

1. What materials will you use for your chair and why?
2. What are your standards for using or rejecting materials or features?
3. What features from other chairs, if any, will you use for your chair?
4. What original features, if any, will you use for your chair?

_____

_____

_____

_____

_____

_____

_____

VISUALIZE: Draw a sketch and make a construction paper model of your chair. Name and describe all of your chair's parts and features.

EVALUATE AND REDESIGN: How close have you come to reaching your goal? Are there ways to improve your design? If so, what are they?

_____

_____

COMMUNICATE: Make improvements if necessary, and present and describe your chair to your class.

☑ Checklist

Review your project and check off each completed item.

_____ Includes information about considered features and why each was included or rejected.

_____ Includes citation of multiple sources used in your research.

_____ Includes a sketch or model of your completed chair, along with written descriptions of its parts and features.

_____ Includes an evaluation of the chair's design and descriptions of any improvements made.

Unit Review

1. Which statements are true of the object shown here? Circle all that apply.

   a. It meets a want or need.

   b. It can be found in nature.

   c. It meets no specified criteria.

   d. It was designed by engineers.

   e. It is an example of technology.

2. Which pair of factors defines any engineering problem? Circle the correct choice.

   a. wants and needs

   b. time and expense

   c. nature and technology

   d. criteria and constraints

3. Fill in the blank with the correct word or phrase to complete each sentence.

A set of criteria	A budget	materials
A list of constraints	criteria	constraints

   _____ states the desirable features

   of a solution.

   Limits on solving a problem are called _____.

4. You are faced with the situation shown here, a filthy pet, and decide to confront it using technology.
Using the numbers 1–8, arrange these steps to show one way you could proceed.

_____ Evaluate test results.

_____ Design a prototype to solve the problem.

_____ Identify the problem to be solved.

_____ Retest the modified prototype.

_____ Construct a final design.

_____ Research existing related technology.

_____ Build and test the prototype.

_____ Modify the prototype.

5. Which steps from the previous exercise are likely to be taken more than once? Circle all that apply.

a. Evaluate test results.

b. Improve the prototype.

c. Construct a final design.

d. Retest improved prototype.

e. Identify the problem to be solved.

6. Fill in the blank with the correct word or phrase to complete each sentence.

> **a single thing**   **several things at once**
>
> **improve their designs**   **develop their criteria**

Testing a prototype works best when the engineer observes

and measures the effects of changing _____.

Engineers test and retest to _____.

7. What makes crash test dummies useful substitutes for human beings? Circle the correct choice.

   a. They are able to avoid collisions.

   b. They have been used since the 1950s.

   c. They contain sensors that collect data.

   d. They are smaller than average humans.

8. Which of the following name good reasons for repeated engineering testing? Circle all that apply.

   a. to ensure safety

   b. to solve problems

   c. to reduce feedback

   d. to eliminate criteria

   e. to develop a final product

9. Fill in the blank with the correct word or phrase to complete each sentence.

failure points	**results**	**prototypes**
working solutions	**design difficulties**	**breakthroughs**

An engineer can find things needing improvement by isolating

_____.

That term refers to _____.

10. Fill in the blank with the correct word or phrase to complete each sentence.

collaboration	**failure**	**research**
a prototype	**peer pressure**	**brainstorming**

_____ gets you a lot of ideas quickly.

However, we say that "_____ leads to optimization,"

because sharing successes often helps make the best engineering solution.

Energy

Explore Online

Unit Project: Truck Pull

How can you use elastic energy or a spring to move a truck? You will design and test a truck with your team. Ask your teacher for details.

Bumper cars show how physical contact transfers energy.

At a Glance

Vocabulary Game: **Guess the Word**

Materials
• Kitchen timer or online computer timer

Directions

1. Take turns to play.

2. To take a turn, choose a vocabulary word. Do not tell the word to the other players.

3. Set the timer for one minute.

4. Give a one-word clue about your word. Point to a player. That player has one chance to guess your word.

5. Repeat step 4 with other players until a player guesses the word or time runs out. Give a different one-word clue each time.

6. The first player to guess the word gets 1 point. If the player can then use the word in a sentence, he or she gets 1 more point. Then that player chooses the next word.

7. The first player to score 5 points wins.

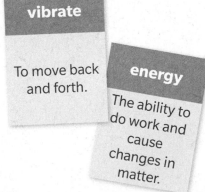

vibrate

To move back and forth.

energy

The ability to do work and cause changes in matter.

Unit Vocabulary

collision: The result of two objects bumping into each other.

electric current: The flow of electric charges along a path.

energy: The ability to do work and cause changes in matter.

energy transfer: The movement of energy from place to place or from one object to another.

energy transformation: A change in energy from one form to another.

heat: The energy that moves between objects of different temperatures.

vibrate: To move back and forth.

What Is Energy?

If you follow an electrical cord from the wall socket, it might lead to a lamp, television, hair dryer, or vacuum cleaner. Many devices use electrical energy to give us other forms of energy, such as heat, light, sound, and motion.

By the end of this lesson . . .
you'll be able to recognize common transformations of electrical energy.

Can You Explain It?

Energy makes things change. Energy in a toaster produces heat, and the heat toasts a slice of bread. Your body's energy might pedal a bicycle so that it goes faster or slows down. Heavy trains need energy to stop and go.

1. Where did the energy come from to make the heavy train speed along the track? When the train stopped, where did the energy go?

_____

_____

_____

_____

_____

_____

_____

_____

 EVIDENCE NOTEBOOK Look for this icon to help you gather evidence to answer the questions above.

Energy Is All Around

Sound? Light? Heat? Motion? ENERGY!

You use energy every day. With energy from your muscles, you move. You pick up a book, open a door, and toss a ball. Using energy from devices, you might talk on the phone, watch a program, or go to school.

Energy is the ability to cause change in matter. Heat energy can dry clothes in a dryer or cook food in the oven. Energy stored in a battery can run a computer. Wind energy can turn a windmill or push a sailboat.

Ways Energy Moves

2. The picture shows different forms of energy. What do you see moving? What energy makes it move? What sends out sound energy? Where is there light or heat energy? On the next page, label each image *energy* or *not energy*.

a. brightly shining sun

_____

d. radio

_____

c. empty shell on the beach

_____

b. rolling water waves

_____

3. Name another example of energy you see in the picture. What kind of energy is it?

_____

_____

4. Choose the best words to complete the sentences.

| light | sound | heat |

Energy is a measure of the ability to cause change in matter. You

can see _____ energy, you can hear _____

energy, and you can feel _____ energy.

5. Language SmArts Choose one of the energy examples above. Describe the effect the energy causes.

_____

_____

Tip

The English Language Arts Handbook can provide help with understanding how to identify cause and effect.

HANDS-ON Apply What You Know

Energy Near You

6. Find five examples of energy in your classroom. Write them below. Group them by the kind of energy they show.

_____

_____

_____

Where Does Our Energy Come From?

When you turn on a television, you see pictures and hear sound. Where do the light and sound energy come from?

You can see a wire connecting a wall socket to the television. That wire carries electric current. **Electric current** is a flow of electric charges along a path. Each photo shows one step in how the energy gets to your home.

Hundreds of millions of years ago, plants took in the sun's energy, just as they do now. After the plants died, a long, slow change turned them into coal. Some of the energy the plants got from the sun is now in that coal. That stored energy is called chemical energy.

a. At the energy generating station, the coal is burned. Burning changes the coal's chemical energy into heat energy.

b. Next, that heat energy makes water become steam, and the steam makes a turbine spin.

c. The spinning of magnets in the generator produces electrical energy from the stored energy within the coal.

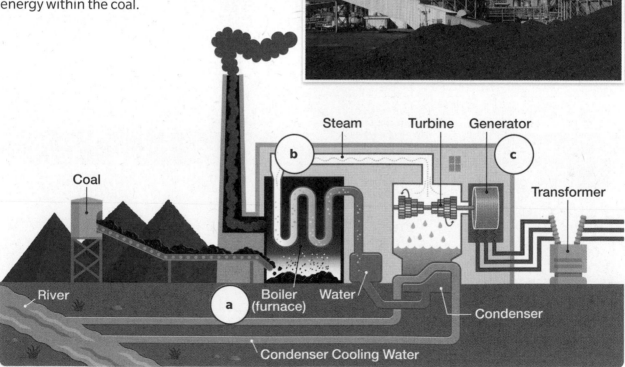

© Houghton Mifflin Harcourt • Image Credits: (tl) ©Guy Jarvis/Houghton Mifflin Harcourt; (r) ©Larry Lee/Getty Images

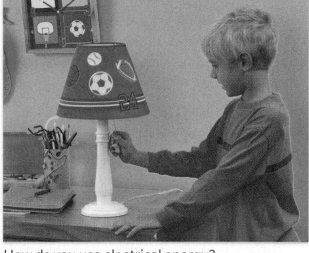

How does that electrical energy get to your home?

How do you use electrical energy?

7. How is the energy we use produced?

_____

_____

_____

Engineer It!
Energy from Algae

Scientists and engineers are always looking for alternative forms of energy for people to use. A new source of energy being developed is the harvesting of algae.

Algae use a gas called carbon dioxide to make energy and release clean oxygen as a byproduct. Algae farmed for this purpose become an oil that is then converted into fuel. These renewable algae fuels are an alternative to fossil fuels such as coal or oil.

Algae are grown in this farm facility.

8. Explain how algae farming can help make air quality better.

_____

_____

 EVIDENCE NOTEBOOK Describe alternative energy, and explain why it is important to have different forms of it.

Saving It for Later

A battery stores chemical energy. When a device uses the battery, the chemical energy inside the battery changes into electrical energy. The device changes the electrical energy into motion, sound, or other forms of energy. There are many types and sizes of batteries for different purposes.

Batteries

9. Learn more about different types of batteries. Then answer the question below.

Explore Online

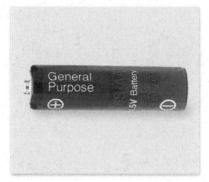

Button batteries are named for their size and shape. They are small and reliable for devices that use small amounts of energy very slowly.

AA batteries are used in many devices. They come in both single-use and rechargeable forms.

9V batteries are useful in devices that change stored energy into other energy. They are a reliable energy source for safety devices.

What type of battery goes in these devices?

_____ _____ _____

Do the Math
Calculate Energy Units

10. Your portable DVD player uses rechargable AA batteries. They last 48 hours before needing to be recharged. In the space below, calculate how many two-hour movies you can watch on your DVD player with fully charged batteries. How many times will the batteries need to be recharged in a 30 day month?

HANDS-ON Apply What You Know

Testing, Testing

11. Suppose you have a battery and you want to know whether it still has energy stored in it. Design a way to test whether the battery still works. Describe your design below.

_____

_____

_____

Putting It Together

12. Choose the words that make the sentences most correct.

| sound | matter | batteries | current |

Energy is a measure of the ability to cause change in _____. You

can feel some heat energy and hear some _____ energy. An

electric _____ is a flow of electric charge. Two ways that energy is

stored are coal and _____.

HANDS-ON ACTIVITY
Light the Bulb

Objective

In a flashlight or other electrical device, a battery may be connected in a circuit. A **circuit** is a closed path or loop that an electric charge flows through.

What question will you investigate to meet this objective?

_____

_____

Procedure

STEP 1 Start by asking questions and sharing ideas. How should you connect the materials you have to make the bulb light up? Plan a simple investigation to find out. Write your plan below, and show your plan to your teacher.

_____

_____

_____

_____

STEP 2 Lay out the parts in the order you think will make the bulb light up.

STEP 3 Connect the parts to test your plan. How did you connect the parts?

_____

_____

_____

_____

© Houghton Mifflin Harcourt

76

STEP 4 Does the bulb light up? If not, keep working until you "see the light"! What did you change about your arrangement?

_____

_____

Analyze Your Results

STEP 5 After you've built a circuit that works, draw a picture of it. Show how the parts are connected.

[blank drawing box]

STEP 6 What occurred when the battery was connected to the light bulb and switch?

_____

STEP 7 What caused the bulb to light up?

_____

STEP 8 What questions do you have about circuits?

_____

_____

Draw Conclusions

STEP 9 Make a claim about bulbs. Cite evidence to support your claim.

_____

_____

Energy Transfer

Transfer to Transform

You walk into a dark room and flip a switch, and suddenly light shines out of a lamp. How does electrical energy become light energy?

The switch allows electric charges to flow through the lamp cord and into the lamp. This is an **energy transfer**, a movement of energy from place to place or from one object to another.

Inside the lamp, another energy transfer moves the electrical energy to the light bulb. The bulb transforms the electrical energy into light energy. **Energy transformation** is a change in energy from one form to another.

A battery is a source of electrical energy. The electrical energy transfers to the flashlight. The electrical energy transforms into light energy.

Electrical energy transfers into the cell phone. The electrical energy transforms into sound energy, which allows you to have a conversation.

Electrical energy from the battery transfers into the mini-drone. The electrical energy transforms into motion energy when it flies away!

Energy from the sun transfers to the solar panels. The solar energy transforms into electrical energy, and the electrical energy becomes heat energy to warm water for bathing and washing dishes.

13. Language SmArts Describe the energy transformation that occurs with an everyday task such as listening to the radio. On a piece of paper, draw a diagram to match your description. Label it.

_____

_____

_____

_____

EVIDENCE NOTEBOOK When the bell rings signaling the end of class, what evidence would you say proves that energy has been transferred?

Many from One

When you turn on a television, electrical energy transfers through the electrical cord into the television. Inside the television, the electrical energy transforms to light and sound energy as well as heat energy.

In the same way, a vacuum cleaner turns electrical energy into motion, sound, and some heat energy. When electrical energy transfers into a device, it usually transforms into more than one form of energy.

Energy Transformations

14. Look at each photo. Write the form of energy the electrical energy changes into after it transfers into each device.

a. When this microwave is running, you hear sounds and see lights and movement. What kind of energy is cooking the broccoli from the inside?

_____

b. The mini-drone is moving. In addition to energy of motion, what form of energy do you hear?

_____

c. The electrical energy transferring into this blender changes into several different types of energy. Which type spins the blade?

_____

d. A hair dryer produces sound and other forms of energy. What kind of energy helps dry your hair?

_____

15. Write the name of each object into each energy form that is present when the object is turned on. Each object will have at least two forms of energy.

> blender   toy drone   lamp
> hair dryer   clothes iron   microwave

Sound	Light	Motion	Heat

16. Language SmArts How can electrical energy be transformed? Conduct research, and list the types or ways electrical energy can transform. Turn your list and research sources in to your teacher.

Changing Forms of Energy

Have you ever been using a cell phone and had the battery "die"? Why do cell phone batteries need to be recharged so often?

Every time a cell phone is active, its stored energy is getting used. Calls use some energy. Using the Internet takes much more energy. Playing games can use up a great deal of energy.

Right after being recharged, the battery indicator shows a full charge.

After the cell phone has been used a lot, the energy stored in the battery is nearly gone.

17. Think of an example from your life of a battery running out of energy. What do you do to conserve battery energy?

_____

_____

_____

_____

Putting It Together

18. Choose the best words to complete each sentence.

| light   sound   motion   heat |

When a hair dryer is turned on, you can feel the blowing

breeze caused by its _____ energy and the drying

warmth from its _____ energy. You can hear the

whir of its _____ energy.

© Houghton Mifflin Harcourt • Image Credits: (l) ©Daviles/Getty Images (r) ©Prykhodov/Getty Images

Discover More

Check out this path . . . or go online to choose one of these other paths.

People in
Science &
Engineering

- **Vampire Appliances**
- **Potato Power**

People in Science & Engineering

Explore
Online

Mayra Artiles, Car Engineer

Have you ever thought of becoming an automobile engineer? Mayra Artiles did, and now she's an engineer working on hybrid electric vehicles. She enjoys designing, building, and testing cars. She even gets to program software into the cars. She likes the teamwork with other engineers, and she also likes getting out to test-drive the cars.

Mayra Artiles pays close attention to transfer of energy. Like any automobile engineer, she knows that the energy of the car's motion affects the battery. Batteries are also sensitive to outdoor temperatures during a hot summer day or in the cold of winter.

Mayra Artiles driving a hybrid car

19. What forms of energy do you notice when a car's engine is turned on?

_____

_____

_____

Dr. Marcus Lehmann

Did you know that people can use the power of ocean waves to generate electricity and fresh water?

The ocean is a fascinating sight for many people. Dr. Marcus Lehmann was so intrigued by the ocean, he decided to use its waves to produce electrical energy.

Lehmann, along with his team of engineers at the University of California, Berkeley, built the wave carpet.

Dr. Marcus Lehmann

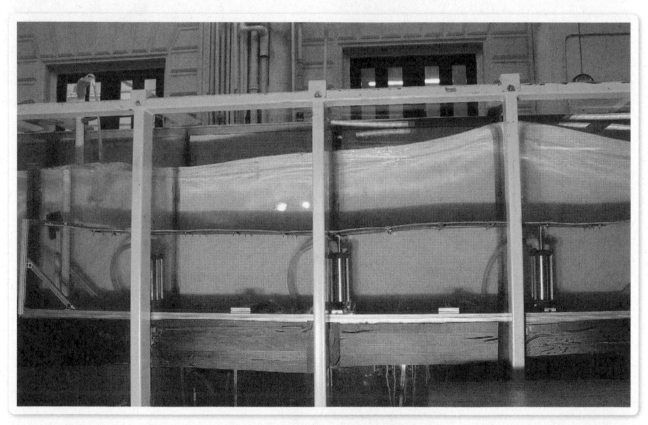

A wave carpet will transform ocean waves into usable energy.

20. Think of an engineering project. What could you design to protect a battery from hot and cold weather? Remember that the protected battery still has to work. It also has to be able to give off some heat while it's working.

_____

_____

_____

Lesson Check

Name _____

Can You Explain It?

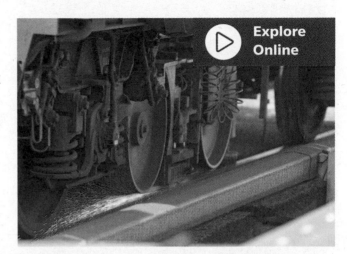

Explore Online

1. You have learned about energy and how one form can change into another. Think back to the photo of the train. Where do you think the energy came from to make the heavy train speed along the track?

   • When the train stopped, where did the energy go?

   • Describe how energy causes change.

   • Explain how energy changes form.

> **EVIDENCE NOTEBOOK** Use the information you've collected in your Evidence Notebook to help you cover each point above.

_____

_____

_____

_____

_____

_____

_____

_____

Checkpoints

2. Which of these shows energy?
   a. a car that has tires
   b. a car that begins to move
   c. a car parked in a garage
   d. a picture of a new car

3. Which of these is a form of energy? Circle all correct answers.
   a. heat
   b. oven
   c. electricity
   d. light
   e. lamp
   f. microwave oven
   g. sound
   h. motion
   i. popcorn maker
   j. chemical

4. What would happen at an electricity generating station if the turbines did not spin?
   a. Coal would not burn.
   b. Motion energy would not generate electric energy.
   c. Chemical energy would not change into heat energy.
   d. Heat energy would not make motion energy.

5. Number these sentences in the order in which they occur.
   _____ Electric energy transfers through the cord.
   _____ Electric energy transforms to light energy.
   _____ You turn on a light switch.
   _____ Electric energy transfers into the lamp.

6. If there is not a complete circuit between a battery and a lamp, what will be the result?
   a. The lamp will turn on, but it will not turn off.
   b. The lamp will turn off, but it will not turn on.
   c. The lamp will both turn on and turn off.
   d. The wires will get very hot.

Lesson Roundup

A. Which of these devices does NOT change electrical energy into motion energy? Choose the best answer.

    a. DVD player

    b. clock

    c. clothes dryer

    d. electric stove

B. Which form of energy can be observed in all of these: a washing machine, a printer, and a radio? Choose the best answer.

    a. sound

    b. motion

    c. light

    d. heat

C. Write each word beneath the intended energy form that is present when the object is turned on. Some objects will have more than one form of energy.

> **blender**   **toy drone**
>
> **hair dryer**   **clothes iron**

Sound	Light	Motion	Heat

D. Choose the best answer.

A cell phone battery will last longest if the phone is mostly used to _____.

    a. text or call

    b. use the Internet

    c. play games

    b. watch movies

How Is Energy Transferred?

A band produces sound energy that is transformed in different ways. Motion energy in an electric guitar, for example, transforms into electric current through wires. This electric energy transforms into sound energy through speakers. The sound transfers through air to reach your ears.

By the end of this lesson . . .
you'll be able to explain energy transfers of light, sound, and heat.

Can You Explain It?

 Explore Online

Wow! Electric drills transfer enough energy to break apart brick walls. People who use electric drills must wear ear protection.

Whispers, on the other hand, can be hard to hear. When people whisper, they have to be close to each other to hear.

1. What is the difference between the sounds in the photos? What do you think makes each sound loud or soft? Explain how energy transfer from loud sounds is different from soft sounds.

_____

_____

_____

_____

_____

_____

 Tip

Learn more about energy and how it is transferred in What Is Energy?

EVIDENCE NOTEBOOK Look for this icon to help you gather evidence to answer the questions above.

Heat

Hot or Not?

How do we know if something is cold or hot? Sometimes, we can see clues. Other times, we can feel whether something is hot or cold. The terms *hot* and *cold* are ways to describe temperature. Heat is energy that transfers, or moves, between objects with different temperatures. Look at these photos that show evidence of energy transfer as heat.

Glassblowing involves high temperatures. Glass is heated by a glassblower to the point that it becomes molten. It can then be shaped. This often involves using a blowpipe to insert air into the glass.

Dry ice is actually a solid form of carbon dioxide. Freezing carbon dioxide takes an extremely cold temperature, much colder than that needed to freeze water. Because dry ice is so cold, it is dangerous to touch.

2. Look at the two pictures. How would you describe the differences? What details in each picture gave you clues?

_____

_____

_____

We use words such as *hot, cold, warmer,* and *cooler* to describe temperature without being exact. To get an exact measurement of temperature, we use a tool called a *thermometer.* Temperature can be measured using different scales in degrees. The thermometer below has two scales, Celsius (°C) and Fahrenheit (°F).

Differences in Degrees

3. This thermometer shows measurements in Celsius (°C) and Fahrenheit (°F). The symbol that looks like a little *o* stands for "degrees." Write a letter in each circle to identify the temperatures shown in the pictures.

Explore Online

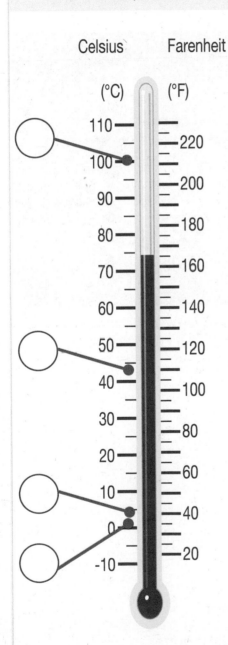

Celsius   Farenheit

(°C)   (°F)

a

The girl's clothes trap heat near her body. Her jacket slows down energy transfer to the cold air. The girl stays warm while playing in the snow in temperatures as low as 0 °C (32 °F) or below.

b

The water coming from this showerhead is hotter than the air near it. We know this because of the steam. The temperature of this shower water is 42 °C (108 °F).

c

The inside of a refrigerator must be kept cold so food doesn't spoil. If it is too cold, fresh food freezes. The ideal temperature is a little below 4 °C (38 °F).

d

Heat moves from the stove to a tea kettle, then from the kettle to the water, and finally from the water vapor to the air. Water boils at 100 °C (212 °F).

Hot by Contact

Remember that heat is energy that transfers between objects with different temperatures. Heat energy sometimes transfers easily between objects that are touching. When objects of two different temperatures touch, heat energy moves from the warmer object to the cooler object.

How does this energy transfer work when cooking a pancake? A pancake griddle starts out at room temperature. When the stove burner is hot, it transfers heat to the bottom of the griddle. The heat spreads through the whole griddle. The heat energy in the hot griddle then transfers to the cooler pancake batter. As the batter heats, the pancake cooks.

Energy is transferred as heat moves from a stove burner toward a pancake griddle.

Energy is also transferred as heat moves from the hot griddle to the colder pancake batter.

4. Select the best words to complete each sentence.

batter	**burner**	**cooler**	**energy**
faster	**griddle**	**slower**	**warmer**

Heat is _____ that moves from a _____

object to a _____ object. A pancake cooks when energy

transfers from the _____ to the _____

to the _____. The last pancake in the batch cooks

_____ than the first pancake because the griddle is hotter.

Distant Heat

Pancakes cook because objects are in contact. The transfer of energy as heat can also occur between objects that are not touching each other.

Study each picture to figure out the heat source. That is, determine where you think the heat is coming from. Then locate the objects the heat is transferring to.

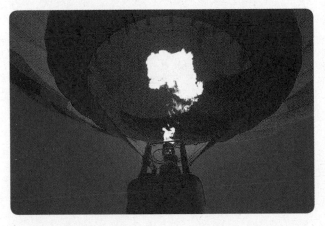

The flame of a gas burner heats the air above the burner. The hot air rises and fills the balloon. Heat transfers into the balloon. Soon the whole balloon is full of hot air.

The space heater transfers heat to the air around it. This makes the air in the room gain heat energy and become warmer. Soon, the room is nice and cozy.

 EVIDENCE NOTEBOOK Sound and heat are both forms of energy. What evidence have you gathered so far to help you explain how sound energy is transferred?

 5. Language SmArts Complete the chart by writing the cause and effect from each example.

Heat Transfer without Touch		
Example	**Heat source**	**What heat transfers to**
marshmallows roasting over a campfire		marshmallows
heat lamp incubating hatching chicks		
snow melting on a sidewalk on a sunny day		

Thermal Imaging

Thermal imaging devices can "see" how hot or cold air moves into and out of a house. By knowing how energy is being transferred, people can insulate areas of the houses to help them stay warmer or cooler.

Thermal imaging devices are also used by fire departments. When there is fire in a house, there is a lot of heat and smoke. Because firefighters cannot see through the smoke, they cannot see if anyone is trapped in a house. By using a thermal imaging device, they can see the cooler bodies in all the hot smoke. This helps the firefighters rescue people and pets from the fires.

Thermal imaging of buildings can help save energy.

6. Two objects on a thermal image are different colors. What must be true of these objects?

_____

_____

_____

_____

_____

Putting It Together

7. Select the best words to complete each sentence.

a different	cooler	does not move	do not touch
transfers	the same	touch	warmer

Heat is energy that _____ when objects have

_____ temperature. Heat energy always moves from

a _____ to a _____ object. A pancake

cooks when objects _____. Heaters warm an area even

though they _____ objects.

Here Comes the Sun

Lighting Up Life

The sun is a star that gives off light and heat. These forms of energy are important to Earth and the things that live on it.

8. What else do you know about energy from the sun? Brainstorm a list of ways in which the sun's energy affects Earth and living things.

_____

_____

_____

_____

All life on Earth depends on light and heat from the sun. The sun heats Earth's atmosphere, making Earth warm enough for water to be liquid and for living things to survive.

Sunlight makes it possible for plants to grow and provide the oxygen we breathe. Plants also provide us with some of our food. The sun's heating of Earth's atmosphere sets the water cycle in motion. Energy from the sun causes wind and weather patterns, too.

Solar panels like these transform light energy into electrical energy that can be used to heat buildings. Solar panels can also change light energy into energy that heats the water used in buildings.

9. Solar panels are evidence for which of these statements?
   a. Light can be transformed into other energy forms.
   b. Heat energy moves toward warmer objects.
   c. Sound transfers heat energy.
   d. Life on Earth depends on sunlight.

A Family of Waves

Light from the sun is a form of energy we can see. These waves travel outward in all directions from the sun and spread out as they move. Other kinds of waves are not visible but also carry energy as they travel and spread out. These other types of energy waves include radio waves, microwaves, and x-rays.

View each image and read the captions to learn about different types of energy waves. Each type of wave has a certain level of energy. The five types of energy waves discussed here are arranged in order of lowest energy (radio waves) to highest energy (x-rays).

Energy Rays

Have you used a microwave oven to heat food? **Microwaves** are higher in energy than radio waves. They have less energy than visible light waves. Images of rain and storm patterns on the weather news online or on TV are also often made using microwaves.

← Lowest energy

Radio waves spread out and travel from a broadcast tower to radio receivers such as car radios. Radio waves have low energy compared to other waves.

Visible light is in the middle of the range of energy waves. Visible light includes all the colors we see. A rainbow shows a range of colors, from red to violet. What we see as red light has the lowest energy of visible light waves. Violet has the highest energy.

© Houghton Mifflin Harcourt • Image Credits: (t) ©Huw Jones/Getty Images

X-rays have much more energy when compared to visible light and radio waves. Have you ever seen an x-ray image of your teeth at your dentist's office? A dentist uses x-rays to better see the health of a person's teeth. X-rays are passed through the body and processed to make images of bones and tissues.

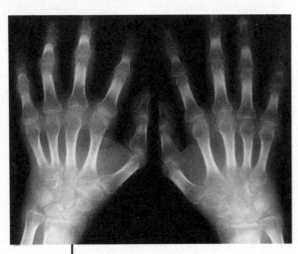

Ultraviolet light is invisible light. Ultraviolet, or UV, light is higher in energy than the range of light humans can see. But some insects can see UV light! The Hubble Space Telescope senses UV light. Images from the telescope show us the UV light given off by many different objects in space.

Highest energy →

 EVIDENCE NOTEBOOK What evidence do you have that visible light is made of all colors?

Language SmArts
Energy Experience

10. Which of the energy waves shown on these pages have you experienced? What evidence do you have of each type of energy?

_____

_____

_____

_____

_____

_____

Enhancing Energy

What kinds of energy transformations happen as the candle burns? Recall that batteries contain stored energy. A candle has stored energy, too. How do we know this? As a candle burns, energy stored in the wick transforms into heat and light. The stored energy changes form. Heat and light are evidence that the candle contained stored energy.

When a candle burns, energy from the wax and wick transforms into heat and light.

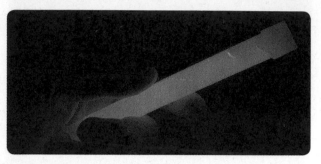

When a glow stick is activated, chemical reactions inside the stick cause the stored energy to transform into light.

11. Choose the best answer to complete the sentences below.

less	microwaves	more	stored energy
ultraviolet light	visible light	x-rays	

Visible light waves have _____ energy than radio waves and

_____ energy than x-rays. One type of energy wave that people cannot see

but some insects can is _____. _____ can be used to make

weather maps. _____ can be used to study bones and teeth. Candles

transform _____ to heat and light.

Putting It Together

12. Choose one type of energy wave, describe its energy level in relation to other waves, and explain one way it is used in everyday life.

_____

_____

_____

Tip

When a question asks you to explain something, use details and examples from the text to support your explanation. See the English Language Arts Handbook for more information.

Design and Test a Solar Cooker

Objective

Collaborate to design and test a cooker that uses energy from the sun.

Design criteria the desired features of a solution. They can include using only certain materials. Or they can be specific to what your solution must do.

Describe the problem that you will try to solve in this activity. How will your solution be helpful in everyday life? What will your solar cooker need to do in order to be a success?

_____

_____

_____

_____

_____

Materials

Discuss with your group what you think you will need to build your cooker. Do some research if needed.

_____

_____

_____

_____

_____

Procedure

STEP 1 List the materials your group plans to use in the **Materials** box above.

STEP 2 Make a sketch of your design for your solar cooker in the box.

STEP 3 Make a step-by-step plan to build and test the solar cooker.

Record the steps your group has agreed upon to build the solar cooker.

_____

_____

_____

_____

STEP 4 Build your solar cooker according to your group's plan. Place the completed cooker in direct sunlight to test it. Use a thermometer to measure how quickly your solar cooker heats up.

Record Your Results

STEP 5 Record temperature changes in your cooker in the data table below.
CAUTION: Do not touch any foil you may have used in your solar cooker when it is in the sunlight.

Solar Cooker Test in Direct Sunlight

Time	Temperature (°C)
0 minutes	(starting temperature)
at 3 minutes	
at 6 minutes	
at 9 minutes	
at 12 minutes	
at 15 minutes	

Analyze Your Results

STEP 6 What was the highest temperature reached in your solar cooker? By how many degrees did the temperature change from the start of the test to the end?

_____

_____

_____

STEP 7 Did your solar cooker meet all of the design criteria you listed on page 99? How well did it succeed in solving the problem you stated? Did all steps of the plan go as expected?

_____

_____

_____

Draw Conclusions

STEP 8 What do you think your group could do to improve the design of your solar cooker? Be specific.

_____

_____

_____

_____

STEP 9 Make a claim about energy transfer from the sun. Cite evidence from your test to support your claim.

_____

_____

_____

STEP 10 List another question you would like to ask about energy transfers.

_____

_____

_____

Seeing Sound

Good Vibrations

Sounds are all around you. But what is sound? Sound is energy that travels in vibrations. To **vibrate** means to move back and forth. Sound vibrations come from an object or organism that starts the vibration. Then, the vibration travels through the air or surrounding objects. When a sound vibration reaches your ear, you sense the sound. Soft sounds have smaller waves than louder sounds.

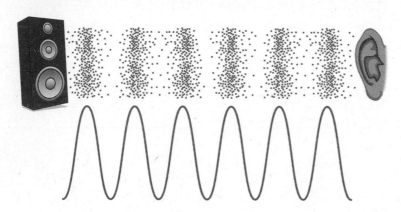

You can't see sound waves. But the small particles that make up all kinds of matter vibrate as sound waves strike objects.

13. Draw a picture to show how sound might move from an object to your ear.

[blank box for drawing]

 EVIDENCE NOTEBOOK Use the information on these pages to help you explain how a loud sound is different from a soft sound.

© Houghton Mifflin Harcourt

When you pluck a string of a guitar, it vibrates back and forth. If you pluck it hard, you transfer a lot of energy to the string. The sound is loud. If you pluck it softly, you transfer less energy. The sound is soft. If the string vibrates faster, the sound gets higher in pitch. If the string vibrates slowly, the sound gets lower in pitch.

Telephones, televisions, radios, computers, and sound systems all have speakers. Speakers transform electrical energy into sound energy. When you listen to recorded music or a video, sound vibrations travel through a speaker. The speaker vibrates and transfers sound vibrations to the air, which then spread outward to your ear.

 HANDS-ON Apply What You Know

Make Vibrations

Can you make sound you can see? Design a musical instrument that allows you to observe vibrations. Below is an example of what you could make.

Use the rubber band to hold a piece of waxed paper around the top of an empty container. The paper should be fairly tight and flat across the top of the container. Place the small objects on top of the waxed paper. Tap the surface of the drum. Observe what happens to the objects.

Materials
- materials of your choosing to make an instrument
OR
- waxed paper
- empty container
- rubber band
- small objects such as grains of sand, rice, or confetti

14. Describe what happened with the instrument you made. What kind of energy transfer did you observe?

_____

_____

_____

_____

_____

Loud and Soft, High and Low

Sounds are everywhere. Some sounds, like whispers, are soft. Other sounds, like jet planes, are very loud. Why do sounds differ? It's the energy transfer. If a lot of energy is transferred from or to an object, the sound is loud. If less energy is transferred from or to an object, the sound is softer. Loud sounds have more energy than softer sounds.

Loud sounds cause particles to vibrate vigorously with much energy. Soft sounds cause them to vibrate with less energy.

Sound Off!

15. Look at the photos. Decide if each sound is soft or loud. Then decide if each has low energy or high energy. Circle your answers.

A plane's engines roar as the plane takes off and touches down.

The airplane makes a (soft loud)

sound, which has (high low) energy.

A mouse is a small animal that makes squeaky sounds.

A mouse makes a (soft loud) sound

when it squeaks, which has

(high low) energy.

When fireworks explode, they produce both sound and light energy.

Exploding fireworks make (soft loud) sounds, which have (high low) energy.

A gentle breeze from an open window can cause curtains to move.

Curtains moving like this make a (soft loud) sound, which has (high low) energy.

Dripping water makes a sound when it hits the floor or ground.

The dripping faucet makes a (soft loud) sound, which has (high low) energy.

16. Select another object or organism that makes sound. Draw it in the box, and describe it as a soft or loud sound, and whether it has high or low energy.

Energy on the Move

Sound vibrations can transmit through any substance. As you can see in the picture below, sound transmits faster through solid materials than through liquids or gases such as air. This is because the particles in solids are closer together than the particles in liquids or gases.

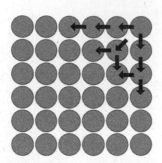 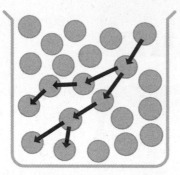 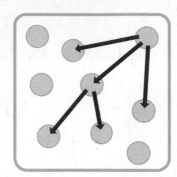

Notice how sound moves in a solid (left), a liquid (middle), and a gas (right). Describe the effect the distance between particles makes.

Do the Math
Compare the Speed of Sound

17. Analyze the data in the table. Order the speeds from fastest to slowest. Then draw a conclusion about the data.

Speed of Sound in Different Materials

Order	Material at 0 °C	Speed of sound (m/s)
	air	331
	copper	4,600
	fresh water	1,433
	rubber	60
	silver	3,650
	steel	6,100

_____

_____

_____

_____

Tuned In!

A tuning fork is a tool that is used to tune musical instruments. When struck, the fork vibrates. When struck, the sound does not travel very far in the air. The sound travels much farther through a solid, because the particles are closer together.

Explore Online

The tuning fork is vibrating in the air.

Here the fork is vibrating against a metal railing.

HANDS-ON Apply What You Know

Tune In

18. Work with a group to test how sound travels through different materials. If you don't have a tuning fork, use something else to make a sound along a metal railing or in the air. On the lines below, list the materials you will use. Describe the steps you will perform to carry out the test. Record your results.

_____

_____

_____

_____

19. Which of these is true? Circle the answer.

   a. Sound vibrations travel faster through air than through metal.

   b. Sound vibrations travel faster through water than through wood.

   c. Sound vibrations travel faster through solids than through gases.

   d. Sound vibrations travel through wood, metal, and air at the same speed.

Energy Bands

You've learned that energy transfer takes place all around us all the time. And a busy kitchen is no exception! Pots and pans bumping against counters, stove burners aglow, and cookies baking are just a few examples of energy transfer in a kitchen.

Look at the photo to find as many examples as you can of energy transferring.

Energy Transfers in a Busy Kitchen

20. Fill in the chart with all the evidence you found in the photo of energy transfers that involve sound, light, and heat in a kitchen. Can you think of others that are not shown in the photo? Add those to the table, too.

Energy Transfers in a Busy Kitchen		
Sound	Light	Heat

Putting It Together

21. Use the following words to write a short paragraph about sound: *vibrations, solids, liquids, gases, soft, loud, more energy,* and *less energy.*

_____

_____

_____

_____

_____

Tip

When you write about things that are different, it is useful to use words such as *than, more,* and *less.* Words ending in *–er* and *–est* are also used in comparisons. See the English Language Arts Handbook for more information.

Discover More

Check out this path . . . or go online to choose one of these other paths.

Careers in Science & Engineering

- **Keep It Cold**
- **The Paynes and Fast-Traveling Whale Songs**

Careers in Science & Engineering

Explore Online

HVAC Tech

What does a heating, ventilation, and air conditioning (HVAC) system do? Many buildings have central heating or air conditioning systems. This means a large fan or pump system blows heated or cooled air through the whole home. But what happens when the system breaks or needs to be serviced? Most people call in an HVAC technician, or HVAC tech for short.

HVAC techs travel around an area to maintain and fix problems in HVAC systems. In cold climates, people need their heating source to work well, especially in winter. The same with cooling systems in a hot climate. When their HVAC system breaks down, people want it fixed fast! An HVAC tech's job involves knowing how to install and fix electrical and plumbing parts of the system.

HVAC systems move air throughout entire buildings.

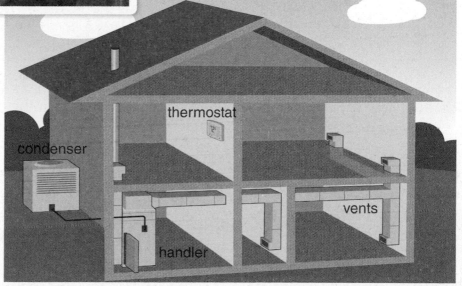

thermostat

condenser

vents

handler

Look at the drawing at the bottom of the previous page . It shows how an HVAC system works. The main unit for the system may be in the basement or in its own closet. The main air conditioning unit may be outdoors or on the roof. A large fan or pump pushes heated or cooled air through sheet metal air ducts or passageways.

An HVAC system may also be used as a fan, by blowing air through the ducts without heating or cooling it. The air ducts guide the air from the main unit to vents leading into each room. The ducts are mostly behind walls, under floors, or above ceilings.

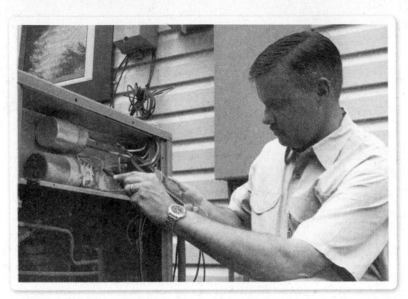

To become an HVAC tech, a person must attend school to get a certificate or be trained by an expert HVAC specialist. Community colleges may offer courses on HVAC systems. Some HVAC courses may be taken online.

22. Suppose you had the chance to interview an HVAC tech. Write three or four questions you would want to ask on the lines below.

_____

_____

_____

_____

_____

23. Interview an HVAC tech or do research to help you answer the questions you wrote above. Write the answers on the lines below.

_____

_____

_____

_____

_____

Lesson Check

Name _____

Can You Explain It?

Explore Online

1. Now that you've learned about energy transfer, explain how sounds transfer energy. Be sure to do the following:

   • Define *sound*.

   • Explain how energy relates to the loudness of a sound.

   • Describe energy transfers in the sounds from an electric drill.

EVIDENCE NOTEBOOK Use the information you've collected in your Evidence Notebook to help you cover each point above.

_____

_____

_____

_____

_____

_____

Checkpoints

2. Which of the following transform stored energy into a useful form? Select all of the correct answers.

   a. battery

   b. candle

   c. glow stick

   d. thermometer

3. Select the words that correctly complete the sentences in the paragraph.

cooler	decreasing	distance
increasing	temperature	warmer

A thermometer shows the _____ of an object. When

temperature rises, it is evidence that heat energy is _____.

When a pancake cooks, energy transfers from the _____

griddle to the _____ batter.

4. Which are evidence of energy transfer involving sound? Select all of the correct answers.

a. a burning candle

b. an airplane taking off

c. water dripping

d. orchestra playing music

e. solar cooker

f. plucking of a guitar string

g. kids whispering

h. Hubble telescope

5. Which of the following involve transformation of energy *into* light energy? Select all of the correct answers.

a. electric light

b. tuning fork

c. solar cooker

d. solar panels

e. burning candle

f. glow stick

6. Circle the type of matter through which sound travels the slowest.

a. wood

b. steel

c. air

d. water

Lesson Roundup

A. Decide which kinds of energy transfer are involved in each example below. Sort each example into the correct column in the table. Some examples might fall into more than one category.

| orchestra | teakettle | solar panels | fireworks |

Sound	Light	Heat

B. Select the best answer to complete this sentence. A good way to use light energy to produce heat is to use a _____.
- **a.** microwave oven
- **b.** battery
- **c.** hand warmer
- **d.** solar cooker

C. Sound will travel fastest through _____.
- **a.** fog
- **b.** air
- **c.** salt water
- **d.** a metal railing

D. Choose the words that make the sentences correct.

| cooler | warmer | high | low |

When a warmer object touches a cooler object, heat transfers from

the _____ object to the _____ object. The

sound of a jackhammer transfers _____ energy, while a

whisper transfers _____ energy.

113

How Do Collisions Show Energy?

These bubble balls allow bumping game players to bump, roll, and flip over without getting hurt.

By the end of this lesson . . .
you'll be able to explain how energy changes when objects in motion collide.

Can You Explain It?

▷ Explore Online

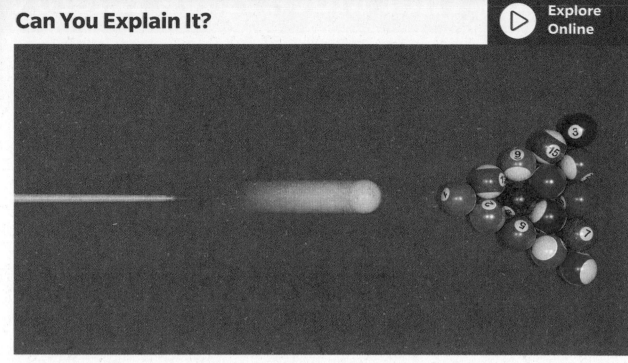

Picture in your mind what happens when the cue ball hits the group of balls at the other end of the table. What happens in a collision?

1. When one ball hits a group of balls, what do you think will happen to the cue ball? What about the balls that were racked up at the other end of the table?

_____

_____

_____

_____

_____

_____

_____

_____

Tip

Learn more about energy in What Is Energy? and How Is Energy Transferred?

 EVIDENCE NOTEBOOK Look for this icon to help you gather evidence to answer the questions above.

Things That Move Have Energy

Energy and Things That Move!

Imagine riding on a huge roller coaster with lots of drops and turns. Are you excited? Are you nervous? Think about inching slowly up the hills—and plunging to the valleys below! But what does this all have to do with energy? Think about the roller coaster and energy in this photo.

Explore Online

The coaster is still as the passengers buckle their seat belts, but it's getting ready to move. As the coaster climbs the hill, it slows down. At the top, there's a pause. As the coaster starts to nudge over the top of the hill, it moves faster. The riders can feel the whoosh of air on their faces as the coaster drops. The coaster's speed changes as it climbs and drops.

2. Does this roller coaster have energy? When does it have energy? How do you know?

_____

_____

What do a moving car, a stretched rubber band being released, and a rolling ball have in common? They all have motion energy! Anything that is moving has motion energy. Objects can also have stored energy, like the roller coaster on the hill, because of their position. That energy beomes motion when it races down!

There might be a dish on the edge of a shelf, ready to fall. Even before the dish falls, it has energy, because of its position up on the shelf.

When you swing on a swing set, you have motion energy. At the top of each swing, you stop moving but have stored energy to move again.

When an archer pulls back on the string to shoot an arrow, energy is being stored. What will happen when the archer lets go of the string?

A rolling soccer ball has motion energy. Kicking it adds to that energy, making it move even faster, and scoring a goal!

3. Choose the best phrase to complete the sentences.

| have motion energy | become motion energy | speed up |

The objects that are moving _____. The objects that are about

to move have energy that can _____.

Swifter and Stronger!

Do you think the speed of an object affects its energy? Look at the pictures. In one, a slow-moving ball strikes a gong. In the other, a fast-moving ball strikes a gong. The more the gong moves, the more energy the ball transfers to the gong.

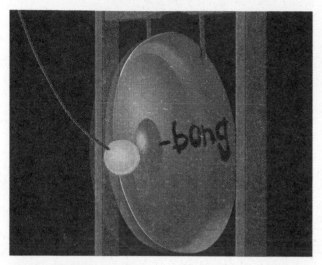

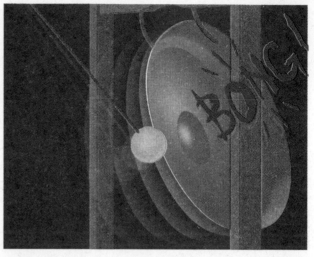

Is the ball swung slowly or quickly? How does the gong react?

Is the ball swung slowly or quickly? How does the gong react this time?

4. Choose the best words to complete the sentences about objects of the same weight.

all	**faster**	**slower**
can	**cannot**	**never**

_____ objects transfer more energy to the object they hit.

_____ objects transfer less energy to the object they hit.

The speed of an object _____ show(s) the amount of energy the object has.

 HANDS-ON Apply What You Know

Bang a Gong

5. Gather materials to experiment with what you have seen in the pictures. Set up the materials and test. Tell how your setup was the same and how it was different. What does this show you about the relationship between speed and energy?

© Houghton Mifflin Harcourt

The Faster They Are Hit, the Harder They Fall

You noticed that the faster you threw a ball, the more energy it had. The increased energy made the gong move more. Now think back to the pool game. If the cue ball moved slowly toward the group of balls at the end, what would happen? What if the cue ball were moving very fast?

A game of bowling is a lot like a pool game. You roll the bowl toward the pins, trying to knock down as many as you can. How does energy change your bowling score? Let's find out!

Slide a bowling ball slowly toward the pins.

When the ball hits the pins, how many pins fall down? Do they topple over or fly from the other pins?

Now move the ball more quickly. How many pins fall?

What else do you notice about the pins when a ball thrown quickly hits them?

6. Use the slow and fast bowling ball example to explain the relationship between speed and energy.

_____

_____

_____

_____

Motion Energy and Size: It's a Big Deal!

You already know that the speed of an object affects its energy. But what about size? If you wanted to knock down bowling pins, would you use a bowling ball or a tennis ball? That's right! You'd use a bowling ball because it's heavier. The heavier ball will have more energy than a lighter ball and will knock down more pins.

Look at the two vehicles. Imagine that they are both moving at 80 km/h (about 50 mph). Which do you think has more energy? If the speed is the same, how does one have more energy than the other?

 HANDS-ON Apply What You Know

Flour Power

7. Try the activity you see in the pictures on the next page. Change one thing you saw. Repeat what was done in the picture, and record your results. How were the results the same, and how were they different? What does this show you about the relationship between speed and energy?

 EVIDENCE NOTEBOOK Explain what would happen to the flour if the balls you used were heavier. Explain what would happen if the balls were lighter.

 **Language SmArts**
Cause and Effect

8. Explain how weight can affect collisions.

_____

_____

_____

_____

_____

Notice the table tennis ball above the pan of flour. What happens when the ball hits the flour? Only a little of the flour moves. The ball didn't have much energy to transfer to the flour.

This baseball is dropped from the same height but is heavier than the table tennis ball. It also falls at the same speed. The crater left by the baseball is larger than the crater left by the table tennis ball. That's because the heavier ball had more energy to transfer.

Putting It Together

9. Explain why there is more damage when objects moving quickly collide than when they are moving slowly.

_____

_____

_____

_____

_____

_____

_____

_____

Test It! Stored Energy in a Rubber Band

Objective

Collaborate to compare amounts of stored energy. You know that energy is stored in a rubber band—but how much energy?

What question will you investigate to meet this objective?

_____

_____

Materials
- safety goggles
- giant rubber band
- chair
- tape
- ruler
- toy car or truck
- meterstick

Procedure

STEP 1 CAUTION: Wear safety goggles. Cut a giant rubber band in half, and tie the ends around the legs of a chair. Place two metersticks in front of the chair. They should be 20 cm apart and in parallel lines to serve as a track for the toy.

What roll does the rubber band play in this investigation?

_____

_____

STEP 2 Tape an index card to the floor behind the rubber band. Mark lines on the card that are 2 cm and 4 cm behind the rubber band. Choose a third distance and mark it on the card.

What do the marks represent?

_____

_____

_____

_____

STEP 3 Place a toy car or truck against the rubber band. Pull the toy back to the 2 cm mark, and release it. Measure the distance the toy travels. Record the data. Repeat this step two more times.

Why do you repeat this step at the 2 cm mark?

_____

_____

_____

STEP 4 Repeat Step 3 using the 4 cm mark and the third distance you selected.

How might your result change if the 4 cm mark had been measured incorrectly and it was actually 6 cm?

_____

_____

_____

STEP 5 Record your results in the table.

Distance Toy Travels					
Rubber band stretched 2 cm		**Rubber band stretched 4 cm**		**Rubber band stretched ___ cm**	
Trial	Distance (cm)	Trial	Distance (cm)	Trial	Distance (cm)
1		1		1	
2		2		2	
3		3		3	

Analyze Your Results

STEP 6 Use the data you collected to answer these questions. Write your answers in the table.

Were your results similar for all the trials with the rubber band stretched back 2 cm? What about 4 cm and the distance you chose?	
If your results were inconsistent across the trials, what do you think caused those differences?	
With which of the stretching distances did the toy travel the longest distance?	
Compare your data with the data of another group. Are the other data the same? If not, why do you think they are different?	

Draw Conclusions

STEP 7 Make a claim about how much stored energy exists in a rubber band based on your experiment. Cite evidence.

_____

_____

_____

STEP 8 Compare the third distance you selected with the other groups in your class. What conclusions can you draw about the distances selected?

_____

_____

_____

STEP 9 What is one question you have about stored energy?

_____

_____

_____

© Houghton Mifflin Harcourt

Wonderful Springs

Ready to GO!

Earlier, you found out that anything that is moving has energy. A ball on top of a hill has the potential to move. When it does, it has energy of motion. You know that if you pull a rubber band back farther and farther, you can let it go—and it will go far! Energy is stored in the rubber band.

Many objects with bands and springs have stored energy that can be released to make them move!

Springtime!

10. Circle the picture that has no stored energy.

At the bottom of the jump, the spring is fully compressed. All the energy is stored in the spring.

As the pogo stick goes up, the energy in the spring is released and becomes motion energy.

At the top of the jump, the spring has transferred all the energy that was stored in it to motion energy.

As the pogo stick compresses, energy is being stored in the spring. The spring has the potential to push up and become motion.

The Bigger, the Better

In the hands-on investigation, you saw that the farther you pulled back the rubber band, the more energy you released to move the car. But what if you replaced the small car with a larger car or one made of heavier steel? How far would the car travel then?

Mass and Energy

11. Take a look at these spring setups. Consider the relative weights of the balls and the relative amounts of stored energy in the springs. Then predict which balls will travel the least distance, the middle distance, and the greatest distance.

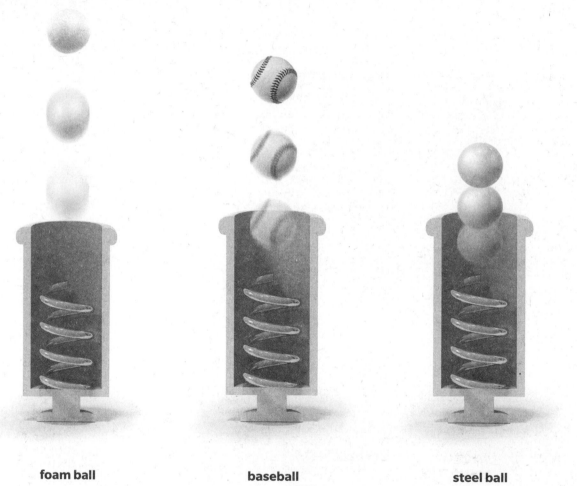

| foam ball | baseball | steel ball |

_____ _____ _____

_____ _____ _____

_____ _____ _____

_____ _____ _____

Engineer It!
Shocking

Buckle up! It's going to be a bumpy ride! When an uneven path causes a vehicle to bounce into the air, the vehicle experiences a collision every time it hits the ground. The motion energy from those collisions jolts the vehicle and the riders inside.

Cars and trucks have springs near the tires. When a spring is compressed, it absorbs and stores energy. The springs in an off-road truck are big and can store a lot of collision energy. That cuts down on the amount of energy that gets transferred to the riders every time the truck hits the ground after bouncing into the air.

12. Describe what it would feel like to ride on a bumpy path in a car that did not have springs to absorb energy.

_____

_____

Language SmArts
Recall from Experience

13. Considering the examples you have seen so far, identify another object that is able to absorb and store energy that is useful to you.

_____

_____

Putting It Together

14. Choose the best word or phrase to complete each sentence in the paragraph.

stored energy	energy of motion	no energy at all	
more compressed	less compressed	lighter	heavier

A compressed spring or a rubber band stretched out both have _____.

An object will travel farther when the compression energy launching it is

_____. If two objects are launched by a rubber band with the same

amount of compression, the object that is _____ will travel farther.

© Houghton Mifflin Harcourt • Image Credits: ©EvrenKalinbacak/Alamy

Collisions

Scatter!

What is a collision? A **collision** happens when two objects bump into each other. Think about a game of pool. When the cue ball hits the other balls, there are collisions. When these happen, energy is transferred. The total energy of all the balls is the same, but energy transfers to make the balls move in different directions. When a cue ball hits one of the balls, its motion slows. It transfers energy to the other balls and then moves in a different direction.

 Language SmArts
Cause and Effect

15. Describe what happens to the other balls that are cued up when the cue ball hits them. Explain the transfer of energy.

_____

_____

_____

If you were going to collide with something, would you rather collide with something moving quickly or slowly? A slow-moving object has less energy, so the collision has less of an impact. A fast-moving object has more energy—so the object it collides with moves fast, too! You can see this in sports. If you want a soccer ball to go fast, you kick it hard!

 EVIDENCE NOTEBOOK You see collisions every day. List some examples in your evidence notebook.

What Happens Next?

Take a look at these images, and think about them. Does a ball move faster and farther in a bunt or with a full swing? What do these images tell you about speed in collisions? View each image to see what happens before, during, and after a baseball collision.

The pitcher sends the ball hurtling toward the plate. The batter puts his bat out to bunt the ball, hoping to make the ball collide with the bat.

The ball has collided with the bat, causing the ball to change direction. It still has motion energy, but the motion of the ball has changed.

The batter has hit the ball. The collision has changed the direction of the ball. The collision has also added more motion energy to the ball.

The outfielder can only watch the ball soar far overhead because the batter has hit a mighty home run.

16. Which collision between the ball and the mitt has the least amount of energy: a caught bunt or a caught fly ball?

_____

_____

_____

_____

Too Hot to Handle!

Have you ever hit a nail with a hammer? That collision makes a lot of noise! What else did you notice about the nail—besides the fact that it went into the wood? If you had touched the nail, it would have been warm. The hammer would be warm, too! What causes the nail and hammer to heat up?

When a screw and wood collide, energy is transferred. Thermal imaging shows a difference in temperature. As the drill pushes the screw, it causes motion and heat energy!

What Happens to Energy in a Drop?

If you took a steel ball and dropped it, some of the energy would go right into the ground. A steel ball isn't springy—it won't bounce much. A tennis ball will. Look at what happens to the energy in a bouncing ball.

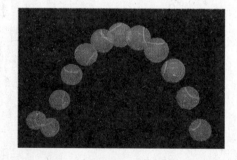

A tennis ball dropped toward the ground bounces back high, but not as high as the height from which it was dropped. Why? Some of the energy is transferred to the ground, and the rest to heat and sound energy.

 HANDS-ON   Apply What You Know

Rebounce

Hold a meterstick perpendicular to the ground. Have a partner hold a tennis ball parallel to the meterstick and drop it. Observe the ball as it bounces. Take turns doing this several times. Where does the energy go when the ball collides with the ground?

Putting It Together

17. What conclusion can you draw about energy transfer based on what you observed with the tennis ball?

_____

_____

Discover More

Check out this path . . . or go online to choose one of these other paths.

People in Science & Engineering

- Bump!
- Collision Game!

People in Science & Engineering

Amanda Steffy

When we drive on roads, we think about the interaction of the tires with the ground. How do we design tires that don't heat up too much? How do we handle roads that aren't perfectly flat?

Now imagine that you design tires for a vehicle on Mars. That's what Amanda Steffy does! She is an engineer for NASA's Jet Propulsion Laboratory (JPL). Her team tests the wheels and tires of the Mars rovers in different conditions. To do this, Steffy and team had to recreate the surface of Mars in California!

Explore Online

Amanda Steffy works for NASA's Jet Propulsion Laboratory.

The tires of the Mars Rover were designed for rough terrain.

131

The surface of Mars is different than what scientists believed it to be. Some of the rocks are sharp and can cut the tires. Some rocks are held tight to the ground while other rocks are very loose.

When a rover tire hits a loose rock, the tire spins faster, but if it hits a sharp rock held tight to the ground, the sharp rock can damage the tire. Amanda tests tires until they fail to find those designs that will hold up on the rough surface of Mars. Understanding these collisions on Earth helps scientists guide the rover on Mars.

Rovers are tested on rough terrain similar to that on Mars.

18. What factors do Amanda Steffy and other scientists who work on vehicles like the Mars rovers need to consider about the energy of motion as they work?

_____

_____

_____

19. How is Amanda Steffy's work related to collisions? Write a few ideas below.

_____

_____

_____

Lesson Check

Name _____

Can You Explain It?

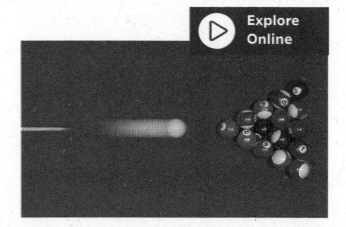

Explore Online

1. What will happen when the ball hits the group of balls? Write a few sentences below to explain what happens to all the balls on the pool table. Be sure to do the following:

   • Describe the motion and collisions.

   • Identify energy transfers.

   • Mention heat or sound.

📋 **EVIDENCE NOTEBOOK** Use the information you've collected in your Evidence Notebook to help you cover each point above.

_____

_____

_____

_____

_____

_____

_____

Checkpoints

2. A soccer ball sits in the grass. A girl pulls her leg back to kick the soccer ball. She kicks! What happens next? Circle all the correct answers.
   a. The ball travels in one direction while the leg continues to travel.
   b. The ball travels in one direction while the leg stops.
   c. The collision of the leg and ball makes the ball travel quickly.
   d. The collision of the leg and ball produces a noise.
   e. The ball travels in one direction while the leg moves backwards.

3. A child plays hopscotch. When she jumps on the ground, which of the following things happen? Circle all the correct answers.
   a. The ground absorbs some of the energy.
   b. The collision produces light energy.
   c. The collision produces heat energy.
   d. The collision produces sound energy.
   e. The girl continues to bounce, going higher each time.

4. Which of the following have energy of motion? Circle all the correct answers.
   a. an electric lamp that has just been plugged in
   b. a child jumping on a trampoline
   c. a fish swimming in an aquarium
   d. the warmth of the sun
   e. a baseball player hitting a ball with a bat

5. A roller coaster moves to the top of a hill where it stops. What happens to the energy when the coaster stops?
   a. The energy becomes motion energy.
   b. The energy is stored energy.
   c. The energy converts to heat energy.
   d. The weight of the roller coaster causes it to collide with another car.

6. An archer is shooting an arrow with a bow. He pulls the string far back, lets the arrow go, and watches it fly far. On his second try, he uses a lighter arrow while pulling the string on the bow back a distance equal to his first try. Tell what happens next. How do you know?

_____

_____

_____

_____

Lesson Roundup

A. You and a friend are sitting on the ground a few meters apart. You each have a basketball and roll them toward each other. The ball that your friend rolls is moving faster. Write a few sentences to tell what happens next.

_____

_____

_____

B. Which of these types of energy changes in a collision? Circle all that are correct.

  a. heat

  b. sound

  c. motion

  d. stored

  e. electrical

C. Which of these is a collision? Circle all the answers you think are correct.

  a. a baseball player bunting the ball

  b. a rubber band snapping

  c. a ball player missing a catch as the ball sails overhead

  d. a hockey player hitting a hockey puck with a stick

  e. two cars driving down a highway

  f. a mallet hitting a croquet ball

D. Choose the phrase that makes the sentence correct.

| tennis ball | bowling ball | table tennis ball |

If a spring is compressed at the same compression and is used to launch a table tennis ball, a tennis ball, and a bowling ball on the same

flat surface, the _____ will go the farthest distance.

ENGINEER IT!
Energy Transfers All Around

The publisher you work for is putting together a book called "Energy Transfers All Around." Your team has been assigned to write a section about how objects transfer energy. To do that, you'll need to set up some experiments, run them, and collect and analyze their data. Then you'll create a multimedia presentation that reports on your procedures, results, and conclusions.

This shows one way to investigate energy transfer. Can you find others?

DEFINE YOUR TASK: What form will your completed project take?

_____

_____

_____

Before beginning, review the checklist at the end of this Unit Performance Task. Keep those items in mind as you proceed.

RESEARCH: Use online or library resources to learn about the principle of physical energy transfer. Search the Internet for simple experiments that explore that principle. Describe and cite your sources.

_____

_____

_____

EXAMINE DATA: Examine the experiments you have found for ideas your team can use to investigate energy transfer. Focus on simple activities using marbles, model cars, or other rolling objects. Tell which approaches seem best to you, and state why.

_____

_____

_____

PLAN YOUR PROCEDURE: Consider the questions below as you plan your procedure and presentation.

1. What materials will you need, and how will you use them?

2. How will your experiment be set up?

3. What will the basic steps of your procedure be?

4. What variables (size and number of rolling objects, speed of movement, etc.) will you introduce into your procedure? How?

5. How will you record, compare, and chart your results?

6. What will be the content, approach, and organization of your multimedia presentation?

_____

_____

_____

_____

_____

_____

PERFORM AND RECORD: Execute your procedures as planned, and record and analyze your results.

COMMUNICATE: Prepare and give a multimedia presentation that describes your team's research, procedures, results, and conclusions.

☑ Checklist

Review your project and check off each completed item.

_____ Includes a clear statement of your task.

_____ Includes a list of cited sources.

_____ Includes a description of your procedure and the materials used in conducting it.

_____ Includes results and analysis of those results.

_____ Includes a multimedia report about your team's research, procedures, results, and conclusions.

Unit Review

1. Which statement best describes the energy transfer shown here? Circle the correct choice.

   a. electrical energy into light and heat

   b. sound and motion into light and heat

   c. light and heat into sound and motion

   d. electrical energy into sound and motion

2. Which of these are forms of stored energy? Circle all that apply.

   a. coal

   b. gasoline

   c. a toaster

   d. a battery

   e. an automobile

3. In your own words, define *energy*. Then name some examples of energy you see every day.

   _____

   _____

   _____

   _____

4. Classify each fuel source as a fossil fuel (F) or an alternative fuel (A).

_____ Solar

_____ Coal

_____ Oil

_____ Wind

_____ Algae

_____ Natural gas

5. An archer shoots an apple from a tree. Number these statements so that they explain the role of energy in that action.

_____ The arrow hits the apple.

_____ The string and bow store the energy.

_____ The archer releases the string.

_____ The apple is forced from the tree.

_____ The archer pulls back on the string.

_____ The arrow transfers energy to the apple.

_____ The arrow's energy moves it through the air.

6. Which choices describe the temperature in the pot above? Circle all that apply.

   a. 0 °C

   b. 32 °F

   c. 100 °C

   d. 212 °F

7. What happens to a cue ball when it collides with another ball during a pool game? Circle all that apply.

    a. It changes direction.

    b. It gains stored energy.

    c. It gains energy of motion.

    d. It loses some of its energy.

8. When a ball is dropped on the ground, it _____ energy with each bounce and eventually becomes _____.

9. Write the sentences in the correct columns.

> **Heat moves from a burner to a pot of water.**
> **Motion energy moves from a hand to a baseball.**
> **Electrical energy changes into light energy in a lamp.**
> **Light energy from the sun changes into electrical energy in solar panels.**
> **Motion energy changes to sound energy in a weather radio.**
> **Heat moves from a hand warmer packet to a person.**

Energy transfer	Energy transformation

10. Write the correct words to complete the sentence.

> heat   temperature

In this picture, _____ is moving between objects of different temperatures.

Waves and Information Transfer

Explore Online

Unit Project: Reflecting Light

How can you bring more sunlight into poorly lit areas in your school? You will plan a method with your team. Ask your teacher for details.

© Houghton Mifflin Harcourt

Cell phones are everywhere! How do your pictures travel from your phone to a phone hundreds of miles away?

At a Glance

Vocabulary Game: Picture It

Materials
- Kitchen timer or online computer timer
- Sketch pad

Directions

1. Take turns to play.

2. To take a turn, choose a vocabulary word. Do not tell the word to the other players.

3. Set the timer for one minute.

4. Draw pictures on the sketch pad to give clues about the word. Draw only pictures and numbers. Do not write words.

5. The first player to guess the vocabulary word gets 1 point. If that player can use the word in a sentence, he or she gets 1 more point. Then that player gets a turn to choose a word.

6. The first player to score 5 points wins.

Unit Vocabulary

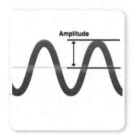

amplitude: Half of the distance from the crest to the trough of a wave.

transparent: Letting all light through.

crest: The top part of a wave.

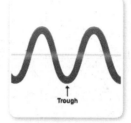

trough: The bottom part of a wave.

opaque: Not letting any light through.

volume: How loud or soft a sound is.

reflection: The bouncing of light waves when they encounter an obstacle.

wave: The up-and-down movement of surface water. It can also be a disturbance that carries energy through space.

translucent: Letting some light through.

wavelength: The distance between a point on one wave and the identical point on the next wave.

What Are Waves?

This American flag waves as hundreds of hands carry it across the stadium.

By the end of this lesson . . .
you'll differentiate between wavelength and amplitude and observe how waves interact.

Can You Explain It?

Imagine you are at the beach and you see a bunch of surfers. They paddle out into the choppy water. When the time is right, they jump up onto their boards and ride the waves back to the beach.

1. How does a surfer know when to stand up on the board to "catch" a wave?

_____

_____

_____

_____

_____

_____

Tip

Learn more about waves and energy in How Is Energy Transferred?

 EVIDENCE NOTEBOOK Look for this icon to help you gather evidence to answer the question above.

HANDS-ON ACTIVITY
✋ Let's Make Waves!

Objective

Collaborate to model the energy transfer that takes place in waves using a coiled spring toy.

What question will you investigate to meet this objective?

_____

_____

Materials
- safety goggles
- yarn
- coiled spring toy
- meterstick
- stopwatch

Procedure

STEP 1 Tie a piece of yarn to the center of the coiled spring toy as shown in the photo above.

Why do you think the yarn is needed?

_____

_____

STEP 2 Put on safety goggles. Take one end of the coiled spring toy, and have your partner take the other. Move so that you are about 4 meters apart.

© Houghton Mifflin Harcourt

146

STEP 3 While your partner holds the end still, slowly wiggle your end of the spring from side to side. In the data table, record how long it takes the wave to get to your partner. Repeat this procedure, wiggling the spring at medium speed and then at a faster speed.

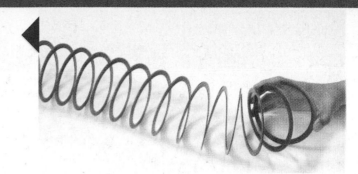

Speed	Time

STEP 4 Hold one end of the spring still. Hold the other end, and gather 10 coils of the spring toy together. Hold onto the last coil, and release the extra coils you gathered. Use the stopwatch to record how long it takes for the wave to reach your partner. Record your data in the first row of the table.

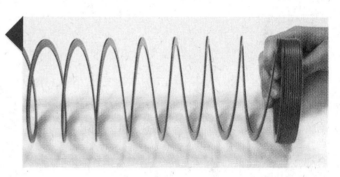

Number of coils	Time

STEP 5 Repeat Step 4 using different numbers of coils. Record the number of coils you gathered and your results in the table under the first row.

How does the number of coils change how long it appears to take for the energy to reach your partner?

_____

_____

Analyze Your Results

STEP 6 How did energy move in your first test?

_____

_____

_____

STEP 7 How did energy move in your second test?

_____

_____

_____

Draw Conclusions

STEP 8 Based on your tests, how would you define a wave?

_____

_____

STEP 9 Use your results to write a claim that relates energy in a wave to the way in which matter moves.

_____

_____

_____

_____

STEP 10 Use evidence from this activity to answer the following question: How do waves move?

_____

_____

STEP 11 What is moving along the spring: waves or matter? How does the yarn provide evidence for your answer?

_____

_____

_____

How Waves Transfer Energy

Waves 101

You may see or experience waves every day. A wave can be the up-and-down movement of water. Wind can make a flag wave. In science, a **wave** is a disturbance that carries energy, such as sound or light.

2. List some other examples of waves in everyday life. How do you know if a wave is strong or weak?

_____

_____

_____

Have you ever thrown a rock into a pond? Once the rock hits the water, it creates a bunch of ripples on the surface. Ripples form because the motion energy of the rock is transferred to the water. Waves are evidence that energy is transferred.

The size of a wave is related to the amount of energy transferred. The rock that was dropped into the pond in the photo was small.

3. What would happen to the waves in this same pond if a larger rock were dropped into the water?
- **a.** The waves would be closer together.
- **b.** The waves would be smaller in size.
- **c.** There would be fewer waves with less energy.
- **d.** There would be larger waves with more energy.

Ocean Waves and Energy Transfer

Waves in the ocean can carry a lot of energy. As a wave gets closer to the beach, the land underneath the water is closer to the surface, causing the energy in the wave to force the water to rise up.

 Explore Online

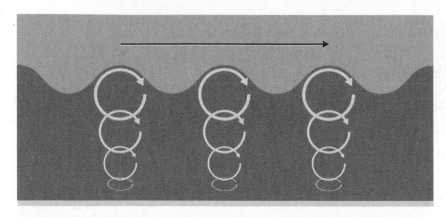

Wind transfers energy to the ocean's surface, causing a wave to form. Each circle shows the movement of water up and around in a wave. Notice that the water doesn't move forward. Only the wave's energy moves forward, as shown by the red arrow.

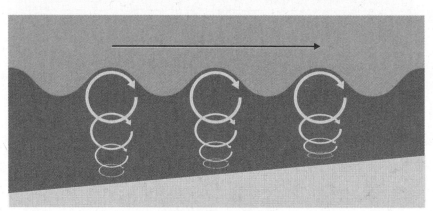

As the water becomes more shallow, the water has less room to move, forcing the water to move higher into the air. The height of the wave increases, and the energy moves forward more slowly.

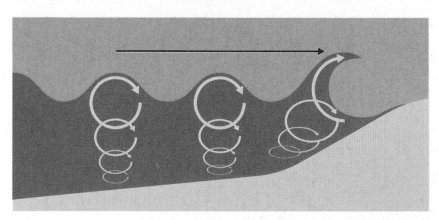

When waves get close to the beach, the back of the wave moves faster than the front, causing the wave to break. All that energy needs a place to go. As the water crashes onto the shore, some of the energy is transferred into sound, and some causes beach erosion.

4. Imagine you are in the ocean. The water reaches your waist. How will energy in a small wave affect you as the wave passes?

_____

_____

_____

If there is a lot of wind or a heavy storm, there is a lot of energy in ocean waves. When they get close to shore, all of that energy is released. Sometimes, out at sea, strong winds create large waves. These waves can travel great distances until they find a place to "break." Surfers often look for places like this so that they can make their way back to shore atop one of these waves.

Buoys are often used as channel markers or as data collection places. While these objects do move up and down with the waves, they do not move forward from their spot. They are often anchored to the sea floor.

Waves crashing along a sandy beach can change the land. Waves add sand to the beach as they come ashore but also erode it and carry it out to sea.

5. Select the best word to complete this sentence.

| energy | motion | buoy |

When ocean waves hit the beach, _____ is released.

HANDS-ON Apply What You Know

Bobbing and Waving

6. Get a bucket and a cork from your teacher. Fill the bucket up part of the way with water, and then drop the cork into it. Notice what happens. Then gently rock the bucket side to side to add more energy to the water. Record your observations of the water in the bucket in terms of energy.

Waves That Move Up and Down

Waves and energy can move in different directions. Sometimes, waves move up and down, like a water wave. Use the pictures below to help you understand waves that move up and down.

Side to Side

7. Use your finger to trace the direction that energy travels. Then trace how matter moves as the wave passes.

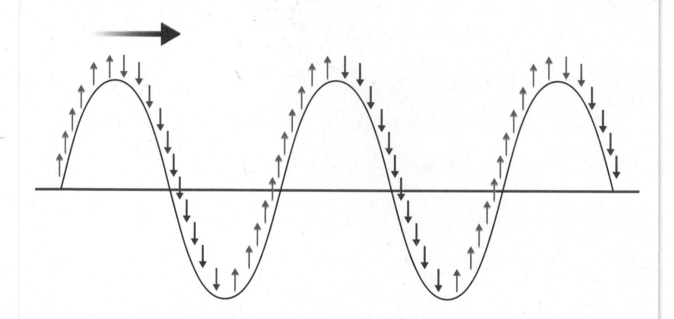

In an up-and-down wave, matter moves at a right angle to the direction of the wave and the movement of energy. Here, the energy is moving to the right.

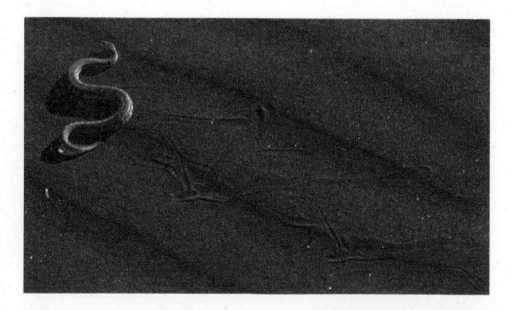

To move forward, some snakes move their bodies from side-to-side. This movement is called *slithering*.

Waves that move up and down or side to side are very common. They can move through all types of matter and even through empty space! As you just learned, water waves are up-and-down waves. The water moves up and down, but the energy moves forward. Sunlight also travels up and down. Light waves can travel through space, where there is no air. Sunlight that reaches Earth warms the planet and everything on it. Study the pictures below to learn more about up-and-down waves.

When people do "the wave" at a game, they stand up and cheer in sequence so it looks like a wave moving through the stands.

Signals from satellites, such as this one, travel through the vacuum of space and through clouds and the air to reach Earth's surface. These waves move at the same speed as sunlight, which moves extremely fast compared to sound waves.

 EVIDENCE NOTEBOOK In an ocean wave, what is moving toward the shore—the water or the energy? What evidence do you have to support your answer?

8. Write a saying that will help you remember how energy and matter move as they travel in an up-and-down wave.

_____

_____

_____

Shake Like a Quake!

BOOM! A firework goes off! There's a bright flash of light followed by the sound of the explosion. Light and sound are both waves. But with sound, matter moves back and forth along the path that the wave travels.

Back and Forth

9. Use your finger to find the three points where the wave is the most compressed. This is the energy of the wave moving to the right.

Explore Online

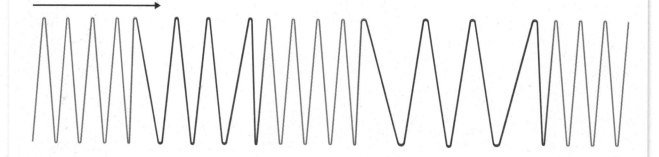

Energy transferred by back-and-forth waves moves in the direction in which the wave moves. Matter moves backward and forward, parallel to the direction the wave is traveling.

When a drum is struck, its skin vibrates. Sound waves traveling away from the drumhead compress and expand the air in bands. In this way, sound energy travels to our ears.

Sound is one example of a wave in which energy and matter move in the same direction. Unlike light, sound can only travel through matter. Sound travels better through water than through air. Because of this, animals that live in the ocean can hear sounds that are far away from them.

Another type of wave that moves back and forth is one of the waves generated during an earthquake. When the ground starts to shake during a quake, different waves move through the rocks in the ground. These waves are used to figure out how strong an earthquake is. Look at the pictures below to find out more about waves that travel back and forth.

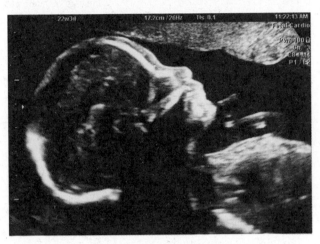

Ultrasound can be used to look inside of things—even people! These sounds move relatively slowly and can't be heard by humans. The sound waves bounce around to form images of objects.

Some earthquake waves make rocks move in the same direction in which the waves are moving. This movement of matter and energy makes the ground shake, and buildings to crumble.

 EVIDENCE NOTEBOOK What types of waves are sound waves? How do they move matter and energy?

 Language **SmArts**
Classifying

Tip

The English Language Arts Handbook can provide help with understanding how to classify groups of items.

10. Classify the examples by writing *up* before the up-and-down waves and *bf* before the back-and-forth waves.

_____ guitar being played

_____ sunlight coming through a window

_____ boat bobbing in the water

_____ ultrasound of a human heart

_____ crowd doing "the wave" at a basketball game

_____ bell being rung

_____ communication satellite in space

Wave Parts

Hunks and Chunks of Waves

Waves have different parts. The top of a wave is called a crest. This is the point on a wave where matter is moved the farthest upward. On a water wave, the crest is the highest point a buoy bobs. The bottom of a wave is called a trough. This is the point on a wave where matter is moved the farthest down. On a water wave, the trough is the lowest point a buoy bobs.

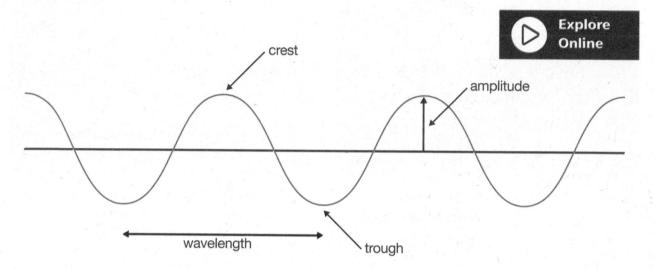

crest

amplitude

▶ Explore Online

wavelength

trough

The distance between adjacent crests or troughs is called the wavelength. The wavelength is the distance between a point on one wave and the identical point on the next wave. The height of a wave is called its amplitude. The amplitude is half the distance from the crest to the trough. The amplitude is related to the amount of energy in a wave. Waves with a greater amplitude have more energy than waves with a lower amplitude.

Language SmArts

Understand Graphics

11. Describe two distances that are the same in adjacent waves.

_____

_____

_____

_____

12. Use the drawings to compare each set of waves. Choose the correct words from the word bank to complete the sentences.

Explore Online

amplitude   wavelength   more   less   shorter   longer

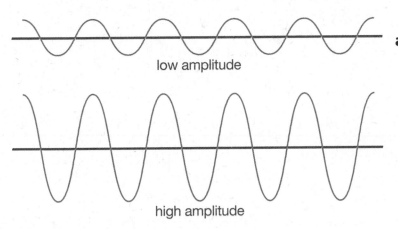

low amplitude

high amplitude

a. The wave on the top has a

smaller _____

than the wave on the bottom.

Thus, the wave on the top has

_____ energy

than the wave on the bottom.

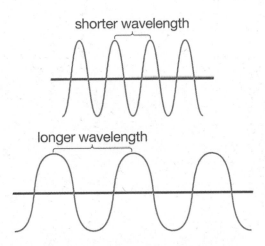

shorter wavelength

longer wavelength

b. The wave on the top

has a _____

_____ than the

wave on the bottom.

13. Select the word or words that make each sentence correct.

crest   trough   wavelength   amplitude

a. The top of a wave is called the _____.

b. The bottom of a wave is called the _____.

c. The distance between two crests is a wave's _____.

d. A wave with much energy has a large _____.

Can You Hear This?

All waves have an amplitude and a wavelength. In a sound wave, the amplitude is related to how loud something is. Loudness is also called **volume.** Compare the sounds described on this page to learn how amplitude differs for different sounds.

Engines on a jet produce very loud sounds. These sound waves have a lot of energy that is carried over a long distance.

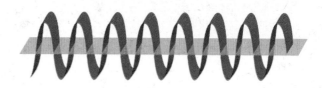

The amplitude of a sound wave produced by a jet engine is very large. The distance between the crest and trough is large.

Songbirds produce soft sounds when they chirp. These sounds can only be heard over a short distance because they have a small amount of energy.

The amplitude of a sound wave produced by a songbird is small. The distance between the crest and trough is small.

Sound waves with more energy and volume have larger amplitudes. Sound waves with less energy and volume have smaller amplitudes. Compare the sounds described on the next page to learn how wavelength differs.

 EVIDENCE NOTEBOOK Write evidence from this page that sound waves have different amounts of energy.

© Houghton Mifflin Harcourt • Image Credits: (t) ©istock / getty Images Plus/Getty Images; (b) ©Malcom Schuyl/Alamy

A dog whistle produces sound waves that only some animals, such as dogs, can hear.

The wavelength of a sound produced by a dog whistle is short. The distance between two neighboring crests is small.

A flute produces a variety of sound waves that humans can hear.

The wavelength of a sound produced by a flute is longer than the wavelength produced by a dog whistle.

Do the Math
Relative Measures

14. Decide which sounds have higher and lower amplitude. Then write each sound in your order of higher to lower amplitude in each column. Be prepared to defend your choices.

a. lion roaring

b. train whistle

c. cat meowing

d. water dripping

e. fireworks exploding

f. flag snapping in the wind

g. trumpet blowing

h. fire crackling

High amplitude	Low amplitude

Surfing the Waves

Remember the surfer from the beginning of the lesson? Let's use what you have learned about the parts of a wave to explain what happens when someone surfs on a wave.

Like all waves, ocean waves have amplitudes and wavelengths. Look at the photo. Which waves should the surfer choose to ride? The larger the waves, the greater their amplitude and energy. The closer the waves are to one another, the smaller their wavelengths.

Putting It Together

15. Select the words that make each sentence correct.

| volume | larger | smaller | amplitude | wavelength |

All waves have _____ and _____. In a sound wave, the amplitude is also called the _____. The louder a sound is, the _____ its amplitude. Sounds that are soft have _____ amplitudes than sounds that are loud.

Waves Interact

Harmony!

Waves can interact with each other. If waves combine in pleasing ways, they are said to be in harmony. Look at the photos on this page to see what happens when waves of sound or light interact.

If you have ever been to a concert, you've heard waves that are in harmony. The musicians here are playing instruments that make different sounds. When the sounds combine, music is produced.

Music is a collection of different sound waves interacting. If you listen carefully to music, you can pick out sounds and notes from each instrument in a band.

If you've been to a theater, you might have seen a dark stage at the beginning of a show. You also may have seen different lights come on, one by one, until the entire stage is lit up.

Like sound waves, light waves can interact, and when many people are seen on a stage and many lights are on, all of the light waves are interacting to show the actors.

16. What are some other examples of waves interacting that you may have seen or heard?

_____

_____

_____

_____

_____

Crossing Invisible Paths

When two waves come together, they can combine to form a wave with larger amplitude. Or they can cancel each other out. Waves can also combine to form a new wave with different characteristics than either of the source waves. Study the pictures and captions on these pages to see what happens when waves combine to add or cancel each other out.

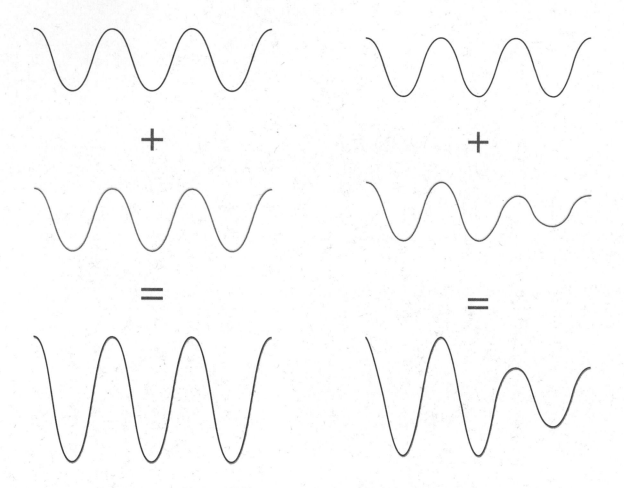

Sometimes waves join together to produce a larger or louder wave. Think about a rock band. When multiple sound waves from the instruments combine, they can create a sound with a loud volume. Waves that are able to combine in this way often have similar or the same wavelength and amplitude.

Waves can also join together to form a completely different wave. The crest of one wave might join with the crest of another wave and create a wave with twice the amplitude. Or the crest of one wave might join with another wave on its way to the trough to form a wave with a much smaller amplitude at that point.

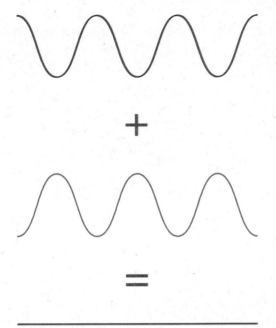

Sometimes waves can work against each other. When this happens, they can cancel each other out. Waves that completely cancel each other out are exactly opposite in amplitude. Then when the two waves join, the lows cancel out the highs to produce no sound.

Noise-canceling headphones are a type of technology that uses wave cancellation. A small microphone outside the headphones picks up background sounds. The headphones then generate a wave with the opposite characteristics. The two waves then cancel each other out. This produces a quiet environment for the user.

 EVIDENCE NOTEBOOK Apply what you've learned on these two pages to ocean waves and surfing.

17. What would happen if two opposite sound waves combined? Choose the correct answer.

    a. The sound would get a lot louder.

    b. The waves would cancel each other out.

    c. The amplitude of the waves would increase.

    d. The wavelength of the waves would get shorter.

Hear the Beat

Do you own a musical instrument? If so, then chances are you know that you need to tune it on occasion. Read on to learn how a piano is tuned.

A piano makes sounds when a key is pressed. That key causes a hammer to hit a string. A piano tuner begins by using a tuning fork, like the one shown in the violin image, to set the pitch for the first note. To do this, the piano tuner loosens or tightens the vibrating piano string until the sound it produces matches the pitch of the sound produced by the vibrating tuning fork. The notes in that octave, or set of notes, are tuned relative to the first note.

Tuning other notes typically involves adjusting the rate, or timing, of beats, which we hear as a series of loud and soft sounds. Beats occur when sound waves interfere, or combine, with each other in certain ways. The piano tuner plays notes together, and changes the timing of the beats that are produced by loosening or tightening the strings. To help time the beats, the piano tuner may use a watch or a clock.

Tuning forks are mechanical.

Some instruments are tuned with electronic tuners.

18. When piano tuners tune pianos using tuning forks, what are they trying to do? Choose the correct answer.

    a. Increase the volume of the instrument.

    b. Decrease the volume of the instrument.

    c. Match the two sound waves.

    d. Cancel out the two sound waves.

Putting It Together

19. Select the words from the word bank to make each sentence correct.

amplitude	louder	quieter	combine	cancel out

Noise-canceling headphones work when sound waves _____.

The headphones _____ unwanted sounds with small

_____ so they cannot be heard. At concerts, waves can

combine to form _____ sounds.

Discover More

Check out this path . . . or go online to choose one of these other paths.

People in Science & Engineering

- **Seismic Waves and Earthquakes**
- **Theater Acoustics**

People in Science & Engineering:

Christian Doppler and Debra Fischer

Why does the siren of an ambulance or fire truck sound different as it gets closer to you? It's the Doppler effect, of course!

Christian Doppler was an Austrian physicist and mathematician. He discovered that sound waves appear to have a higher pitch as you approach the object making the sound. Pitch is the highness or lowness of a sound. When an object giving off a sound wave is moving away from you, the sound will appear to have a lower pitch. This is called the Doppler effect.

Christian Doppler

▷ Explore Online

Imagine a fire truck is approaching you, siren blaring. As the truck passes you, the siren will have a lower pitch. The reason is the time it takes for the wave crests to reach you increases when the truck is moving away. So, from your point of view, the wavelength is longer and thus the pitch is lower.

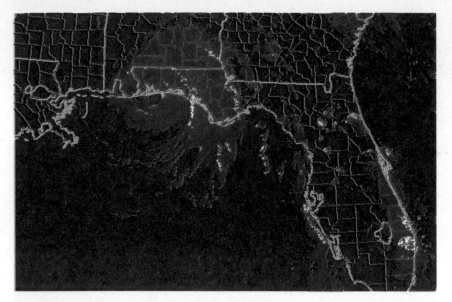

Doppler's ideas are used by weather forecasters to predict oncoming storms. Using Doppler radar, they are able to see how fast storms are moving. They can also determine where the storms are going and what types of precipitation are going to fall.

There are many uses for the Doppler effect. The Doppler effect helps identify and predict the movement of storms. It helps locate new planets, too! Although you can see stars all over the sky, you cannot see planets orbiting them.

Dr. Debra Fischer, an astrophysicist, is one scientist who uses the Doppler effect to find planets. Dr. Fischer uses a telescope fitted with special equipment to detect changes in the frequency of light from a star, caused when an unseen planet pulls the star toward, and then away from, Earth. The shifts in the frequency of starlight produced by these slight gravitational "tugs" are like the apparent changes in the pitch of sounds produced by objects moving toward and away from an observer.

Dr. Debra Fischer

Dr. Fischer has also used the Doppler effect to calculate the size of planets, and she is helping to provide astronomers with instruments they can use to detect smaller planets that are farther away from the stars they orbit.

20. On the lines below, describe the Doppler effect.

_____

_____

Lesson Check

Name _____

Can You Explain It?

Explore Online

1. Now that you have learned about waves, explain how a surfer gets onto a wave. Be sure to do the following:

   • Explain how waves carry energy.

   • Identify the properties and parts of waves.

   • Identify what happens when waves interact.

EVIDENCE NOTEBOOK Use the information you've collected in your Evidence Notebook to help you cover each point above.

_____

_____

_____

_____

_____

_____

_____

_____

_____

Checkpoints

2. Choose the words that make each sentence correct.

   | quickly | slowly | small | large | energy |

   If a spring is wiggled _____, the amplitude of the waves that form is

   _____. This is because the amount of _____ of the wave

   is small.

3. Write *high* or *low* on each line to correctly describe the amplitude of each sound.

_____   _____   _____   _____

4. In the second column of the table, write *long* or *short* to correctly describe the wavelength of each wave.

surfing wave	
seismic wave	
tuba	
dog whistle	

5. Which of the following are examples of wave interactions? Select all that apply.
   a. a full orchestra playing a song
   b. moving a spring back and forth quickly
   c. having two spotlights on a performer
   d. watching a movie in surround sound
   e. tuning a piano to the correct notes
   f. wearing noise-canceling headphones on an airplane

6. Choose the words or phrases that make each sentence correct.

cancel	separate	noise-canceling headphones	theater spotlights

_____ are devices that _____ out

unwanted sounds. _____ are devices that also show how waves

can interact. When only one of these objects is used, waves do not combine.

Lesson Roundup

A. Which of these are evidence that ocean waves have energy? Select all of the correct answers.

    a. They can combine or cancel each other out.

    b. They need a medium in which to move.

    c. They make things wet.

    d. They crash when they hit shore.

B. Which of these are true? Select all of the correct answers.

    a. All waves move up and down.

    b. Some waves don't need a medium in which to travel.

    c. Some waves lack troughs and crests.

    d. All waves move back and forth.

    e. Some waves transfer energy and some transfer matter.

C. Label each part of the wave.

    a. crest   **c.** wavelength

    b. trough   **d.** amplitude

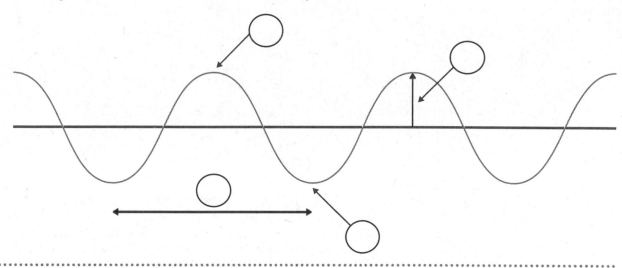

D. What else have you learned about waves in this lesson?

_____

_____

_____

_____

How Does Light Reflect?

Even astronauts take selfies! All visible light bounces off certain surfaces, such as mirrors. Light bouncing into our eyes allows us to read these words.

By the end of this lesson . . .
you'll be able to explain how light interacts with different surfaces and why people can see the things they do.

Can You Explain It?

▶ **Explore Online**

Telescopes like this one can be used to capture light from objects in space. This nebula, which is a cloud of dust and gases, is millions of kilometers from Earth. So how can we see it?

1. How does a telescope allow us to see things that are millions of kilometers away from us?

_____

_____

_____

_____

_____

_____

_____

_____

_____

Tip

Learn more about waves in What Are Waves? and how energy transfers through waves in How Is Energy Transferred?

 EVIDENCE NOTEBOOK Look for this icon to help you gather evidence to answer the question above.

Disappearing Coins

Objective

Collaborate to investigate light's affect on objects. Have you ever tossed coins into a fountain and made a wish? If so, then you have probably noticed that sometimes you can see the coins in the water and sometimes you can't. Is this magic? Not really. It has to do with how you see light and how it can bend.

What question will you investigate to meet this objective?

_____

_____

Procedure

STEP 1 Place a few pennies into a shallow baking dish.

STEP 2 Slowly walk backwards while keeping an eye on the pennies. Stop when you can no longer see them over the side of the pan. Mark your spot on the floor with masking tape.

What is the masking tape for?

_____

_____

STEP 3 Slowly add water to the pan until it is just about full. Make sure the coins stay in the same place.

Why do the coins need to remain in the same spot?

_____

_____

STEP 4 Stand on the spot you have marked on the floor. Look at the coins in the pan. Draw what you observe below. Use lines that show how light moves from the coins to your eye. Drain the water from the dish and have your partner repeat this activity.

Analyze Your Results

STEP 5 How did what you and your partner observe change when the water was added?

_____

_____

STEP 6 Stick a pencil straight down into the pan. Look at it from the side of the pan. What do you see? What does this tell you about how light moves?

_____

_____

Draw Conclusions

STEP 7 What can you claim about light in making the coins visible?

_____

_____

STEP 8 Does light always behave in this way? Cite evidence to explain your answer.

_____

_____

Reflection and Our Eyes

What Do You See?

Imagine you are in a windowless room. There are no lights. Can you see anything? Of course not! Why? You need light to see. Light travels from place to place as a wave. It may come from the sun, a candle, or a flashlight. Once light reaches its target, it might pass through the target. Or it may bounce back. Read these pages to find out more about light.

Most people close the window blinds in their bedrooms at night to make the room darker. By not letting light into the room, many people can sleep through the night.

When window blinds are open, light can enter the room. People need light to see things. With the blinds open, much of the outside light can enter the room.

2. Why can't you see outside with the blinds closed?

_____

_____

_____

_____

This box allows light to pass through it. The box is **transparent,** which means light can pass through it. A car window can be transparent also.

This box is **translucent,** meaning some light can pass through it but is scattered so no clear image is visible. Waxed paper is also translucent.

This box prevents any light from passing through it. The box is **opaque,** which means light cannot pass through it. Most window blinds are opaque.

All, Some, None

3. On the lines, identify each material as *opaque, translucent,* or *transparent.*

_____

_____

_____

_____

_____

_____

EVIDENCE NOTEBOOK What type of material is a telescope mirror? How does it interact with light?

Bouncing Waves

Look in the mirror. What do you see? Your reflection looking back at you! A **reflection** is the bouncing of waves when they hit an obstacle. Anything you can see is either a light source or is reflecting light. In the case of your reflection, the obstacle is the back surface of the mirror.

So how does a mirror work? A piece of glass is polished, and then painted with shiny silver paint on one side. When light hits the layer of paint, it is reflected. Many other things can reflect light, too.

Common Reflectors

4. View the images and read the captions to learn more about some surfaces that reflect.

Mirrors cause light to bounce off them. The image in a mirror is backwards because of the way the light reflects from the mirror.

A disco ball is made of many tiny mirrors. When light hits them, it reflects and makes colored spots on the walls.

Some of the sunlight that hits solar panels is absorbed and some is reflected. Solar panels change sunlight into electricity.

Water is a good reflector of light. Sunlight is bouncing off water in this lake. When the lake is perfectly still, the water can act like a mirror.

Not all reflective surfaces are flat. This sculpture is called Cloud Gate. It is located in Chicago, Illinois. Even though it is not flat, it is very smooth, and light can still bounce off its surface.

As you have read, light can be reflected off of different surfaces. And the surface does not have to be flat to reflect light.

The color of an object can also impact how light is reflected. Dark objects usually do not reflect as much light as light-color objects. If you are out after dark, you want to be sure to wear light-color clothing. This way, car headlights will reflect off your clothes and allow drivers to see you.

5. Identify three other things that reflect light. How do you know they are reflecting light waves?

_____

_____

_____

_____

_____

Smooth Waves Ahead

You've learned that many surfaces are smooth and reflective. However, not all smooth things reflect light. There are some surfaces that look smooth to the eyes and even feel smooth to the touch. But when those surfaces are magnified, you can see they are very bumpy. This may impact the surface's ability to reflect light.

Look at the photos on these pages to see how some everyday objects look under a microscope. Even though some objects may appear smooth, their surfaces are really bumpy. The bumps scatter light in different directions making an object less reflective.

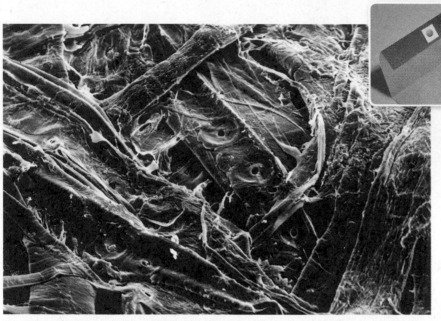

A piece of paper feels smooth to the touch but is actually very bumpy! The bumps scatter light.

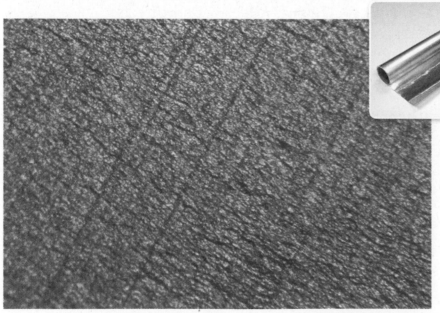

Aluminum is a metal that is used for many things, including foil used in the kitchen. It has a very reflective surface.

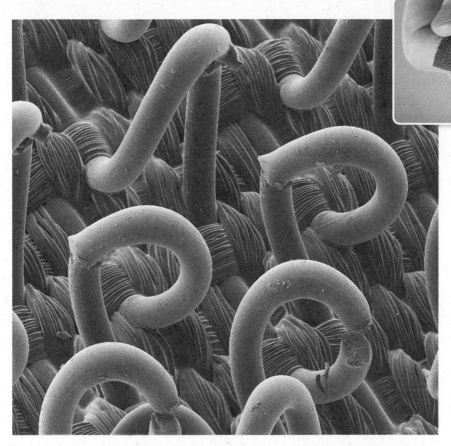

Hook-and-loop fasteners help objects stick together. They are not reflective.

Gold is a metal often used to make jewelry. The surface of gold is usually reflective.

6. Which three objects will *best* reflect light?

a. a mirror

b. a black T-shirt

c. a brown piece of paper

d. a stapler

e. a piece of aluminum foil

f. a gold necklace

From the Sun to Your Eyes

You know that to see something, there has to be light. Your eyes are specially adapted to collect as much light as possible. Imagine you're outside on a sunny day, playing catch with a friend. You can see your friend standing a few meters away. You can see the object she's tossing to you. All of this is possible because light is bouncing off everything and entering your eyes.

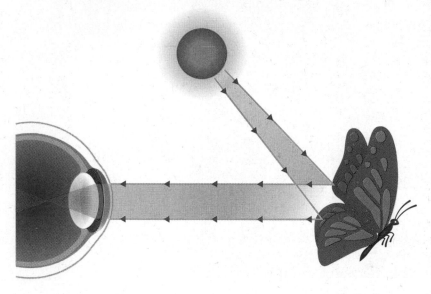

In order to see an object, it must be emitting light, like the sun, or light needs to bounce off it. What happens on a sunny day? Light from the sun reaches Earth. The light reflects off an object. Then, the light hits the surface of the eye.

7. What would happen to the path of light if it hit a transparent surface like a glass window?

   a. The light would change direction.

   b. The light would reflect off it.

   c. The light would pass through it.

   d. The light would scatter all around.

HANDS-ON Apply What You Know

Seeing Color

8. How do colored filters change the way we see? Using transparent colored light filters, observe the clothing of your classmates. What does a red shirt look like through a red filter? Does a green shirt appear the same through the same red filter? Make a chart to describe what different colors look like through the filters. What patterns do you see in your data?

Let's Make Colors!

Light is made up of many different colors all blended together. Each color of the rainbow has a different wavelength. As a result, you see a red apple as red because the red wavelengths are being reflected by the apple's skin. The other wavelengths are absorbed by the apple.

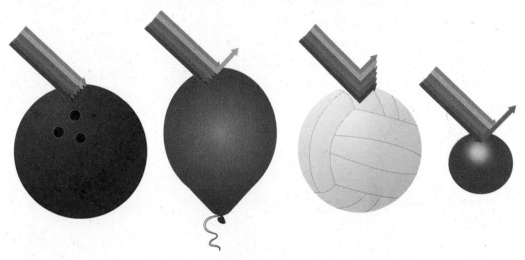

These four objects are reflecting and absorbing light differently. The bowling ball is absorbing all wavelengths of visible light. The blue balloon is reflecting blue wavelengths but absorbing all the others. The volleyball is reflecting all wavelengths. The orange is reflecting orange wavelengths but absorbing other wavelengths of light.

9. Look at the object to the right. Explain how it is absorbing and reflecting visible light.

_____

_____

_____

Putting It Together

10. Select the words to correctly complete each sentence.

> **white   black   opaque   transparent**

Light reflects from _____ surfaces and passes through

_____ ones. _____ objects reflect all

wavelengths of light. _____ objects absorb all visible light.

HANDS-ON ACTIVITY
Reflecting on Angles

Consider This Have you ever been to a carnival that had a fun house? Sometimes these places have fun mirrors. When you look into them, your reflection can be squashed, stretched out, or even pencil thin. How do these mirrors work? Well it all has to do with the reflection of light. These mirrors are bent in a certain way. This bending changes the angle at which light hits them to make the funny images you see.

Materials

- 10 cm × 10 cm piece of cardboard
- small mirror
- modeling clay
- 3 pushpins of different colors
- labels
- metric ruler
- protractor

Objective

Collaborate to investigate how angles of reflection affect light.

What question will you answer during your investigation?

_____

_____

_____

Procedure

STEP 1 Stand the mirror up at the end of the cardboard using the clay.

STEP 2 Label the pushpins PP1, PP2, and PP3. Place PP1 and PP2 into the cardboard 5 cm from the mirror.

Why does the position of the pushpins matter?

_____

_____

_____

STEP 3 Position yourself so that PP1 lines up with the reflection of PP2.

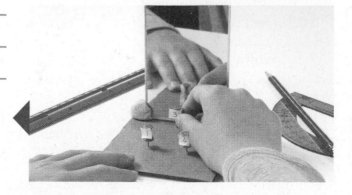

STEP 4 Put PP3 into the cardboard at the end of the mirror in front of PP2's reflection. PP1, PP3, and the reflection of PP2 should make a straight line.

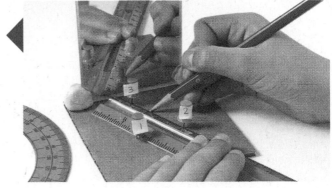

STEP 5 Draw lines on the cardboard to connect PP3 with PP1 and PP2.

STEP 6 Draw lines along the front of the mirror and then remove it.

STEP 7 Use a protractor to measure the angles between each of the PP lines and the mirror line.

Why did you remove the mirror during this step of the investigation?

_____

_____

_____

_____

STEP 8 Draw a picture of your cardboard as seen from above. Include the point each pin forms as well as the angle formed by the pins.

Analyze Your Results

STEP 9 What shape did the lines make when you recorded their angles? Why?

_____

_____

_____

STEP 10 Why was it important to start this activity with PP1 and the reflection of PP2 in the same line?

_____

_____

_____

Draw Conclusions

STEP 11 Use evidence from this activity to make a claim about how light travels and behaves when it strikes an object.

_____

_____

_____

_____

STEP 12 What effect would moving one of the pushpins farther from the mirror have on the angle?

_____

_____

_____

STEP 13 What are some other questions you have about how light reflects from a surface?

_____

_____

_____

_____

Refraction and Lenses

Seeing Light

Light moves faster than any other wave or object, but its speed can change. Light moves much faster in air than it does in the water. When light hits a liquid like water it bends.

The sun is millions of kilometers away from Earth. Thus, it takes time for its light to reach us. The sunlight you see at any time left the sun eight minutes before you see it!

White light is made of different colors of light. So when white light shines through a prism or passes through raindrops, it is separated into the colors of the rainbow.

Do the Math
Convert Units of Time

11. The sun is millions of kilometers from Earth. When light leaves the sun, it takes eight minutes to reach Earth. It takes sunlight 12 minutes and 40 seconds to reach Mars. How much longer, in seconds does it take sunlight to reach Mars?

© Houghton Mifflin Harcourt • Image Credits: (l) ©digis/Shutterstock; (r) ©GIPhotoStock/ Science Source

Breaking Straws

Think back to the Disappearing Coins activity. The coins were not visible from a distance when the pan had no water. Once water was added, the coins were visible. This was an optical illusion caused by refraction.

Refraction is the bending of light waves as they pass from one material to another. Light changes direction and speed when it hits a barrier. Look at the photos to see how refraction can affect how things appear.

12. Why does the straw in the photo appear to be bent?

_____

_____

_____

_____

_____

_____

An archerfish is able to see insects on plants that are above the water. When the fish hunts for food, it watches an insect to set up its attack. To capture its prey, the fish squirts water out of its mouth, at just the right angle to account for refraction. The water hits the insect and knocks it into the water.

To better understand refraction, think about the following. A group of students is walking in a straight line and at a fast pace.

When the students reach a line drawn on the ground, they slow down, which also causes them to change direction. Every time a student crosses the line, he or she does this.

These students represent light waves. The line on the ground is the boundary between any two materials. The shift is the refraction caused when the waves change direction and speed.

Language SmArts
Using Word Parts

13. Use a dictionary to divide the words *reflection* and *refraction* into parts. Write original definitions for each word using the definitions of its parts.

_____

_____

_____

14. Chose the words to correctly complete each sentence.

| broken | medium | refraction |

_____ is the bending of a light wave. This happens

when the wave changes _____. This interaction can

make objects appear _____.

Lenses

Some objects, such as cells, are too small to see with the unaided eye. Other objects, such as stars, are too far away. Over time, many tools have been invented to help people look at objects they otherwise would not be able to see.

Many of these tools contain lenses. A lens is a piece of plastic or glass that magnifies an object. Some lenses are curved; others are flat. Read on to find out more about how lenses have helped us.

Smile!

15. As you read about this camera, underline key phrases to help you remember how a camera such as this one works.

Have you ever used a camera? If so, you may know that it has several important parts. Cameras need light to take pictures. This light gets manipulated by the lenses in the camera. After the light comes through the lenses, it bounces off a mirror, reflects two more times inside a prism, and then forms an image in the eye piece.

The lens of this camera is a collection of curved pieces of glass that magnify an image. Larger lenses are able to refract more light than smaller lenses.

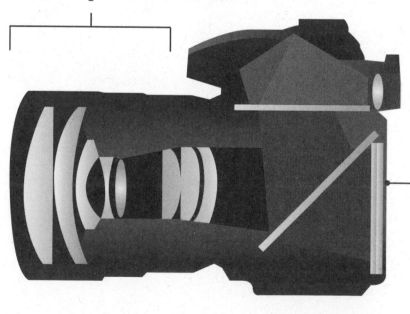

The mirror in this camera reflects the light that enters through the lenses and moves it toward the viewfinder. The mirror flips up just before a picture is taken.

 EVIDENCE NOTEBOOK How do lenses and mirrors affect light?

Imagine you are out at sea on a boat. You see something in the distance but can't make out what it is. You take out your binoculars to get a better look. Binoculars are useful for seeing things that are far away. They use a series of lenses to collect and bend light to magnify an object. They work a lot like telescopes but are not as powerful.

Now imagine being at the park. You find a small pebble that has a bunch of shiny flecks in it. You want to get a better look at them, so you pull out your hand lens. Hand lenses are sometimes called magnifying glasses. They're great tools to use to see small things. They have curved lenses that change how the light goes through them to make things look bigger.

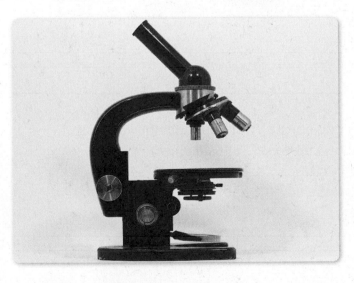

You know that there are many creatures on Earth too small to see with an unaided eye. But did you know that there are parts of these creatures that are really, really small? To see these small creatures and their parts, you could use a microscope. Like binoculars and hand lenses, microscopes use lenses to make objects look larger than they really are.

16. Which of the following refract light to produce images of objects? Select all that apply.

a. binoculars

b. hand lenses

c. windows in a house

d. car windshields

e. microscopes

f. mirrors

Human Lenses

You know that to see something, there needs to be light. Your eyes have special parts that collect visible light so that you can see the world around you. Just like a camera or a telescope, each of your eyes has a lens. The job of the lens is to focus the light.

Remember that light travels in a straight line to your eyes. Once the light enters your eyes, it goes through different parts of your eyes and brain before you see an image. Because light moves so fast, this process happens nearly instantly.

From the Sun to You

17. Use the information above, the drawing, and the information below to answer the question.

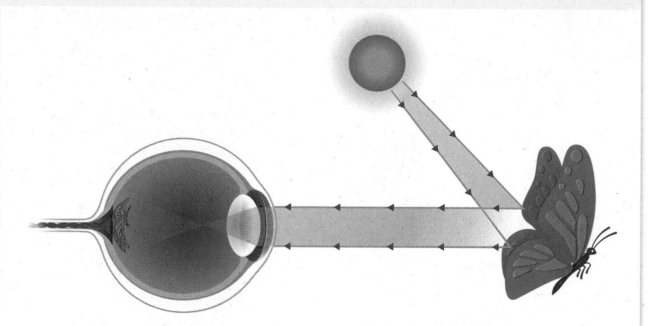

Light leaves the sun and then reflects off of an object. The reflected light hits the surface of the eye and travels through the lens to a focal point inside the eye. There the light is changed into signals and sent to the brain. The brain figures out the signals, and you understand what you see.

What happens at the focal point inside the eye?

_____

_____

18. Write or diagram the process that produces vision into a flow chart showing six steps.

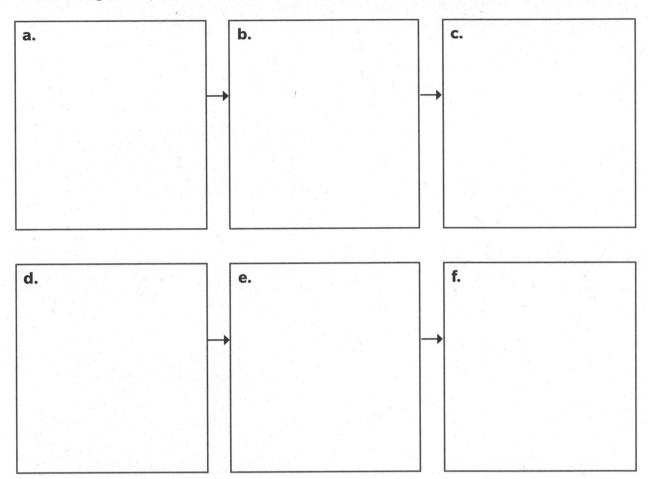

a.

b.

c.

d.

e.

f.

19. Choose the words to correctly complete each sentence.

| air | brain | eyes | light |
| spine | reflects | refracts | |

In order to see, _____ must be present. Light

_____ off of objects and enters the _____.

There it is changed into a signal that is passed to the

_____. The signals are used to produce an image.

This is how you see things.

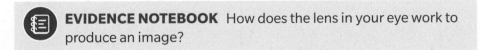

EVIDENCE NOTEBOOK How does the lens in your eye work to produce an image?

Super Lenses

You probably know a few people who wear glasses to help them see. Eyeglasses are lenses used to correct vision problems. The two main types of lenses used in glasses are convex lenses and concave lenses. Both lenses allow light to pass into them, but each interacts with light in different ways. Study the drawings to see how these lenses compare.

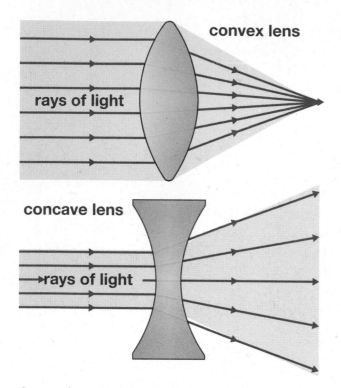

Convex lenses are curved outwards. Concave lenses are curved inwards. Notice how these differences cause light to behave once it enters the lenses.

Eyeglasses are often used to correct vision problems. Some people do not have to wear glasses until they are older. Others start when they are young.

20. Use the information and drawings to complete the table below to compare and contrast convex and concave lenses.

Convex	Both	Concave

Read This!

21. Get a convex and a concave lens from your teacher. Use each lens to look at different types of printed materials. Place one lens over the words on a worksheet or this book page. Note whether the words appear larger or smaller. Then use the other lens and do the same thing.

How does the print look different with the different lenses?

_____

_____

_____

Telescopes can be used to see things that are millions and millions of kilometers from Earth. Telescopes may use lenses, mirrors, or a combination of both to gather and bend light. A refracting telescope has a curved primary lens that gathers light and bends it. It then sends the light waves to another lens called the eyepiece. This is the part through which you look. A refracting telescope bends light to produce a magnified image of a distant object.

22. Choose the word or phrase to correctly complete each sentence.

bend	bounce off	concave
convex	far away	close up

_____ lenses focus light into a single point.

_____ lenses cause light to spread out. Refracting

telescopes cause light to _____ and are used to view

objects that are _____.

Engineer It!
Designed for Safety

Have you ever noticed words printed on the passenger-side mirror of a car? The message says: *Objects in mirror are closer than they appear*. What does this message mean?

These side mirrors might appear flat, but if you examine them very closely, you can see that they have a curved surface. They are slightly convex.

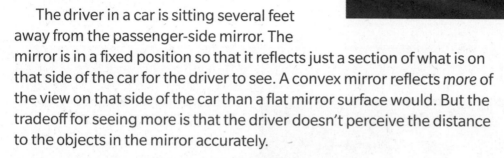

The driver in a car is sitting several feet away from the passenger-side mirror. The mirror is in a fixed position so that it reflects just a section of what is on that side of the car for the driver to see. A convex mirror reflects *more* of the view on that side of the car than a flat mirror surface would. But the tradeoff for seeing more is that the driver doesn't perceive the distance to the objects in the mirror accurately.

Why does this matter? One of the things a driver uses mirrors for is backing up a vehicle. If a driver is backing a car *toward* an object in the mirror, it is important to know that the object is closer than his or her eyes might think!

23. If a convex car mirror makes objects appear closer than they really are, what do you think the reflection in a concave mirror would look like?

_____

_____

Language SmArts
Identifying Main Ideas and Details

24. Identify the main idea of the passage on this page. Then write down at least three details that support this idea.

_____

_____

_____

_____

_____

© Houghton Mifflin Harcourt • Image Credits: (tr) ©Patrick Strattner/fStop/Getty Images

Discover More

Check out this path . . . or go online to choose one of these other paths.

People in Science & Engineering

- **Light and Art**
- **Lighthouses and Lenses**

People in Science & Engineering:
Optics Engineers

Microscopes, telescopes, and lasers are all tools that make use of light, mirrors, and lenses. Without knowing how light behaves, none of these would have been invented.

People who design tools that use light are called *optical engineers.* They investigate how light refracts and reflects. They use this knowledge to invent tools that can be used in many different fields. For example, lasers are beams of light that can be used to carry out a delicate surgery. Lasers are also used to scan products at the checkout counter or produce a light show at a rock concert.

Optical engineers, like Dr. Kristopher Davis, use knowledge of light and lenses to help engineers design useful tools, such as video projectors, laser printers, or even the Hubble Space Telescope.

Optical engineers at the University of Central Florida developed technology to test the efficiency, or the ability to produce electrical energy with less waste, of solar cells like this.

Like with most fields of research today, optical engineers commonly use computers to design models. They also use computers to test their models. In this field, it is important to have a very strong background in both math and science.

A few of the latest discoveries coming out of this engineering field include a communications cable that can carry 22 times more signal than regular cables. Another discovery is flexible glass that can be used in the fields of communications and energy exploration. These discoveries, along with many, many others, will lead the way as the technology and optics age continues.

Dr. Davis and the UCF optics team use LEDs with different wavelengths of light attached to a system of fiber optic cables to test solar cell efficiency. By understanding how efficient a solar cell is, optical engineers can alter and improve their design, so they produce more electrical energy.

Optical engineers at UCF also conduct research on lasers like this one, fiber optics, and optical imagery for medical fields. The goal of each research field is to improve our every day lives with optical materials that are stronger, faster, and more efficient.

25. Research other aspects of optical engineering. What kind of training does someone need to become an optical engineer? Would you enjoy working in this field? Why?

_____

_____

_____

_____

_____

Lesson Check

Name _____

Can You Explain It?

Explore Online

1. Now that you know about lenses and how they interact with light, explain how a telescope allows us to see things millions of kilometers away. Be sure to do the following:

   • Describe how light moves.

   • Explain how light reflects and refracts.

   • Detail how light allows you to see objects.

> 📓 **EVIDENCE NOTEBOOK** Use the information you've gathered in your Evidence Notebook to help you cover each point above.

_____

_____

_____

_____

_____

_____

_____

Checkpoints

2. You shine a light into a dark container. The light shines back at you. Which of these terms describe the container and behavior of the light? Select all that apply.
   a. reflection
   b. refraction
   c. opaque
   d. transparent
   e. translucent

3. Choose the word or phrase that correctly completes each sentence.

bend	destroy	stay in place	move
angles	heights	eye	brain

Water can _____ light. Coins thrown into a fountain look

like they _____ when looked at from different

_____. This is because the water creates an illusion. Your

_____ is tricked into thinking the coins have moved.

4. You put a spoon into a clear glass of water. When you look at the spoon, it appears bent. Which of these describes the glass of water and the behavior of the light? Select all that apply.

a. reflection   **d.** transparent

b. refraction   **e.** translucent

c. opaque

5. You shine a flashlight into a glass of apple juice. Some of the light bounces off the liquid. Some of it passes through it. Which of these describe the juice and the light behavior? Select all that apply.

a. reflection   **d.** transparent

b. refraction   **e.** translucent

c. opaque

6. Label each object as *opaque, transparent,* or *translucent*.

_____   _____   _____

Lesson Roundup

A. You throw a penny into a fountain. You see where it lands. Your little brother cannot. He is standing next to you. Which of these explains why this is so? Select all that apply.

   a. Light was reflected.

   b. Light was refracted.

   c. He's at the wrong angle.

   d. The water is opaque.

   e. The water is too cold.

   f. The penny is reflecting light.

B. Order the steps to show how light from the sun allows you to see an object.

_____ You see the object.

_____ Light is changed into a signal.

_____ Light leaves the sun.

_____ Signal enters the brain.

_____ Light reflects off of an object.

_____ Light enters the lens in your eye.

C. Choose the word or words that correctly describe each object and how light behaves in the situation.

reflection	refraction	passes through
opaque	transparent	translucent

_____   _____   _____

D. Which of these describes a lens that causes light to spread out when it focuses it?

   a. translucent

   b. opaque

   c. concave

   d. convex

How Is Information Transferred from Place to Place?

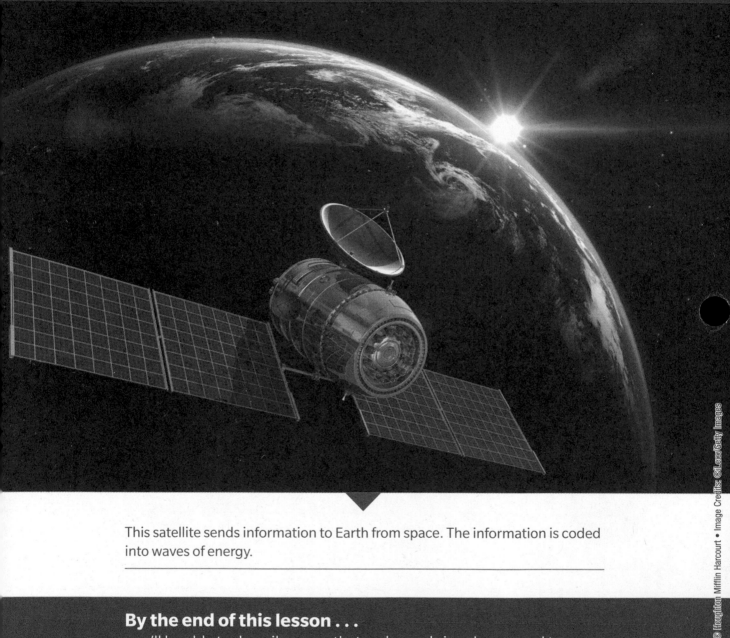

This satellite sends information to Earth from space. The information is coded into waves of energy.

By the end of this lesson . . .
you'll be able to describe ways that codes and signals are used to transfer information.

© Houghton Mifflin Harcourt • Image Credits: ©iLexx/Getty Images

Can You Explain It?

▶ Explore Online

How times have changed! 30 years ago, televisions were large pieces of furniture and telephones had wires. Today, we have televisions that have hundreds of channels, and phones that can take photos and surf the web.

1. How has the way we receive information changed over the years?

_____

_____

_____

_____

_____

_____

_____

_____

_____

_____

_____

Tip

Learn more about energy transfer in What Are Waves?

 EVIDENCE NOTEBOOK Look for this icon to help you gather evidence to answer the question above.

History of Information Transfer

The Old Ways

Humans always have needed to communicate. Before talking, ancient people probably sent messages by pointing, grunting, or hand gestures. As different groups of people spread out, they needed to communicate over distances. Also, it became common for ancient cultures to record their histories using pictures.

One of the earliest recorded forms of communication used *pictographs*. These drawings are often painted in caves. They are very fragile but have lasted because they are painted in places that are protected from the weather. Pictographs recorded events, such as important ceremonies and good hunting areas.

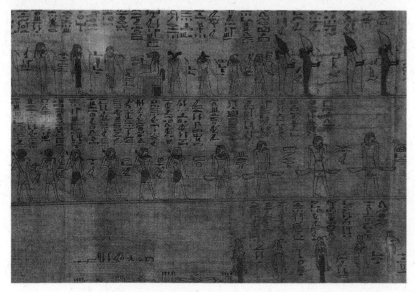

Ancient Egyptians communicated using *hieroglyphics*. Hieroglyphics are symbols for ideas, words, or letters. For example, a drawing of a lion might represent the letter *L*. Egyptians made papyrus, an early form of paper, so ideas were not limited to the size of a wall. They passed on information about ceremonies. Because hieroglyphics could be written on paper, they could be carried from place to place.

2. Language SmArts Interview an older adult. How have the ways they communicated changed over time?

How can people send messages long distances without making any noise? In ancient China, there were often battles that involved soldiers from faraway places. Soldiers used smoke signals to communicate across long distances.

Native Americans on the plains in the Midwest also used smoke to send signals. The smoke signals served as a "universal language" between the tribes.

A talking drum has two heads. It can be tuned to different notes, but usually produce low wavelengths. Drums were used to tell stories, send messages, and lead ceremonies. Drums are an ancient form of communication, but they are still important to the cultures of West Africa.

"One if by land. Two if by sea." So goes the story from Paul Revere's ride, letting people know the British were coming. Using the lanterns in the Old North Church, colonists were able to send simple messages to many people at once.

3. Choose the words or phrases that make each sentence correct.

| hieroglyphics   lanterns   talking drums   smoke signals |

One of the earliest ways of sending messages was through the use of

_____. This involved drawing pictures on paper. To send signals

across long distances, the ancient Chinese used _____ to alert

the troops that enemies were coming.

Newer Ways

With the discovery of electricity, signals could be sent over much greater distances, thousands of miles away. A device called the *telegraph* was invented that allowed information to travel all over the world along wires. The telegraph was invented in the 1830s. A man named Samuel Morse invented a "language" that could be used to send messages using the telegraph.

International Morse Code

Character	Morse code	Character	Morse code	Number	Morse code
A	·—	N	—·	1	·————
B	—···	O	———	2	··———
C	—·—·	P	·——·	3	···——
D	—··	Q	——·—	4	····—
E	·	R	·—·	5	·····
F	··—·	S	···	6	—····
G	——·	T	—	7	——···
H	····	U	··—	8	———··
I	··	V	···—	9	————·
J	·———	W	·——	0	—————
K	—·—	X	—··—		
L	·—··	Y	—·——		
M	——	Z	——··		

The telegraph code is called *Morse code.* It is a series of dots and dashes, each making up a letter. An operator in one place taps out a message. It travels through wires to another location. A second operator decodes the message. Operators needed to be skilled so messages could be sent quickly and accurately.

 4. Language SmArts Telegraph messages were very popular, but not always reliable. Research how telegraphs were sent. Name some ways a message might be miscommunciated or misunderstood.

_____

_____

_____

_____

© Houghton Mifflin Harcourt • Image Credits: (r) ©North Wind Picture Archives/Alamy

By using the telegraph, messages have been sent all over the world. When it was first invented, cables were laid across the Atlantic Ocean to Europe. This was beneficial during the World Wars to keep track of enemies. The last telegraph message was sent in 2013.

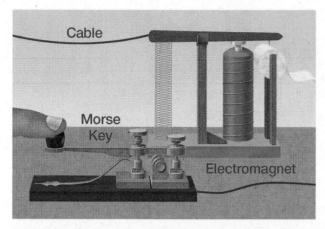

A battery, an electromagnet, a telegraph key, and a cable make up a telegraph. By tapping the key, an electric pulse is sent through the cable.

The telegraph operator uses a code called Morse code. It is a series of dots and dashes, each making up a letter.

The signal moves along the cable to a machine on the other end.

The electric pulse is transformed into sound. The operator listens and decodes the dots and dashes, and makes words from them.

5. In the space below, write your name in Morse code.

Codes

Think about sending a signal. Each message needs a sender and a receiver. Chances are you talk to or text your friends using the phone. Or you have a face to face chat in the lunchroom at school.

How do you make your message clear? Sometimes, using text messages does not always get the correct message across. If you use shorthand like symbols or emojis, the receiver may not know what you mean.

Sometimes you want to send a message that's meant for only one person. How do you keep it a secret? In this case, you want to be sure only the receiver can understand the message. To do this, you could use a secret code. Secret codes have been around for hundreds of years. They are really useful to protect important information, like bank accounts or personal information on websites.

6. Can you think of some times in history when a secret code would have been needed? What makes a good code?

_____

_____

_____

_____

During World War II, the United States government needed a way to encode special messages. They recruited Americans who spoke little known Navajo as code talkers.

Another tool used to send secret messages is the *Enigma machine,* a device that looks a lot like an old typewriter with a keyboard and some wheels sticking out of the top. The Germans developed the Enigma during World War II.

 EVIDENCE NOTEBOOK Why was the Navajo language perfect for a code to use against the Japanese in World War II? Record your answer in your Evidence Notebook.

As you have seen, there are many different codes. Codes and different ways to send codes have been around for thousands of years. But codes don't have to be very complicated, and they can be fun to use. Look at the images to see some more codes.

Flags can be used to relay coded messages, especially between ship and shore, or two people too far away to hear each other.

A **scytale** is another tool that can be used to send a coded message. A strip is wrapped around a tube. A message will be added, then the tube removed.

HANDS-ON Apply What You Know

Make a Scytale

7. Get some paper, scissors, tape, pencil, and paper towel tube from your teacher. Cut the paper into long strips. Tape one end of the strip to the side of the tube. Wrap the rest of the strip around the tube. Write a message from one end of the tube to the other. Then add a bunch of other letters around the ones you wrote to fill in the space. Take off the strip of paper and trade it with a classmate to see if they can figure out what you wrote.

Putting It Together

8. Suppose you wanted to send a secret message using Morse code. Circle the things you need to send a complete message. Select all that apply.

   a. a sender

   b. a microphone

   c. a series of dots and dashes

   d. a pile of papers

   e. a tablet

   f. a receiver

Pixels to Pictures

Objective

Have you ever looked closely at a picture using a magnifying glass? If so, you may have seen that the image was made up of millions of tiny dots. Each dot that makes a picture is called a *pixel*. When there are a lot of pixels in an image, it will be very sharp. If there are few pixels, the image will be blurry.

> **Materials**
> • pencil/pen
> • paper
> • ruler
> • markers

Discover how pixels work.

What question will you investigate to meet this objective?

_____

_____

Procedure

STEP 1 Use the ruler to draw a grid on the paper. It should have 7 columns and 11 rows.

STEP 2 Fill in the boxes with ones and zeros as seen in the illustration on the next page.

STEP 3 Color in the boxes that have ones in them to see what the message says.

STEP 4 What does the message say?

_____

_____

0	0	0	0	0	0	0
0	0	0	0	0	0	0
0	1	0	1	0	1	0
0	1	0	1	0	0	0
0	1	0	1	0	1	0
0	1	1	1	0	1	0
0	1	0	1	0	1	0
0	1	0	1	0	1	0
0	1	0	1	0	1	0
0	0	0	0	0	0	0
0	0	0	0	0	0	0

Analyze Your Results

STEP 5 Each box in the grid represents one pixel. What was the hardest part about making an image using pixels? What was the easiest?

_____

_____

_____

STEP 6 How are the ones in your grid used to represent something else?

_____

_____

_____

STEP 7 Using a new grid, make a message for a friend to decode. To show more details, should you include more boxes in the same size grid or fewer?

_____

_____

_____

Draw Conclusions

STEP 8 The pictures on a computer or television screen are made of pixels of colored light. What has to happen to those pixels for the pictures to show things that look like they are in motion?

_____

_____

_____

Bits and Bytes

Bits of Code

In our digital world, everything needs to be changed into code. Pictures, words, and numbers on our devices are converted into codes of ones and zeros that can be sent as electronic signals. This collection of ones and zeros is called *binary code*. Each number of the code is a bit. This is the smallest piece of information that can be stored by a computer. Binary code is a little tricky at first. However, once you get the hang of it, it is pretty easy.

Binary code

Binary code is needed to store information in a computer. If you were to look at the software that runs your phone, gaming system, or laptop, you would find nothing but a very, VERY long chain of ones and zeros.

HANDS-ON Apply What You Know

Make Your Own Code

9. Using what you learn about binary code, make your own set of binary cards. Get index cards from your teacher and then draw a different number of dots on each one. The first card should have one dot. The second card should have two, and so on, up to 16. With a partner make binary code for a number and then decode what it is.

Learn Binary Code

1

Look at the cards. Starting with one on the right, the next card would be 2, then 4, then 8, then 16, then 32, then 64, and so on.

2

If the first card is showing its dot, it is a one. If the card is not, it is a zero. An example with four digits of a binary code would be 0001.

3

The binary number for two would be 0010. Here, the two-dot card would be flipped over showing its dots. All the others are hidden.

4

The binary number for three would be 0011. Here, both the two-dot card and the one-dot card are flipped.

Do the Math
Code Blue

10. In the table below, turn each blue number into binary code.

Number	Number of "dots" per bit					Binary code
	16	8	4	2	1	
1	0	0	0	0	1	00001
3	0	0	0	1	1	00011
5						
10						
13						
19						
21						

Connecting the World

Today, a lot of what we do is made easier by wireless technology. We are able to talk on a cell phone. We can "stream" movies to our TVs from wireless Internet modems or to our handheld devices. We can even listen to music that is relayed as signals from satellites.

All of these things rely on electronic signals transferring bits of code from one place to another. However, these signals can be interrupted. If you have ever had a dropped cell phone call or an Internet video that would not play, you have experienced an interrupted digital code.

The number of bits a device can move or process is a constraint. If a signal has too much information for the network to move, it slows down or stops. This is why you hear about the need for an Internet connection to be high speed.

Today we listen to music on our phones and other small devices.

11. What types of things can cause the picture to buffer on the computer or TV?

_____

_____

_____

_____

12. Language SmArts Think about two criteria and two constraints to a device that can surf the Internet.

_____

_____

_____

_____

What is happening here? Error messages appear often on computers and tablets. Sometimes it means there was a communication problem between parts of the system. Other times it means that the stream of bits of code needs to catch up.

Find the Cause

13. Draw a line from the issue to the possible cause. Find a cause for each issue.

too much traffic online

too far from
cell tower

error message

computer speed is
too slow

lost signal

too many phones
being used at once

 EVIDENCE NOTEBOOK How do you know when your cell phone signal strength is low? What can you do to improve it?

Code, Computers, and Networks

Humans communicate with words, letters, numbers, and pictures. Computers and other devices do not know what these are. Instead, they need to translate them into code (remember binary code?).

Now picture how signals are sent between computers. First, you input the words on the keyboard. Then, the computer translates them into binary code. If you are sending an email or a text to a friend, the computer needs to be able to "talk" to the Internet. The way computers talk to the rest of the world is with a device called a modem.

The modem sends the signals to and from your computer. When you send an email, the pathway goes from your computer to the modem. It then goes to another modem and then to your friend's computer.

Kesha just sent an email to her grandma. The signal goes from the computer to the modem. It goes across the lines to grandma's modem and then to her computer.

Grandma is waiting for Kesha's email. To get to her, the signal comes from her modem. It takes very little time for the message to be received.

How Computers Help Us Communicate

Suppose you want to send a email. How does it work? The sending computer translates a message into codes that can be sent.

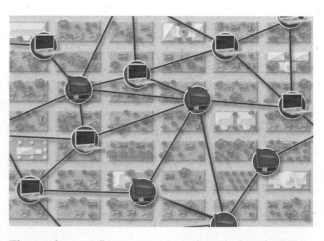

The codes are first sent through your local area network, or LAN, made up of all the modems in a virtual neighborhood.

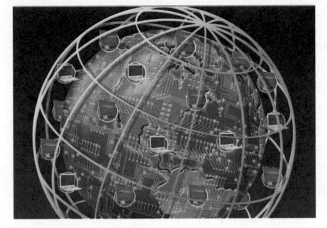

The LAN sends the signals to all the computer networks to the internet.

The signals containing coded words and pictures are decoded clearly by the receiver. Your message can now be read.

14. Language SmArts Put these steps in order of how a message would get from Kesha's computer to Grandma's computer.

Kesha's modem	keyboard	Grandma's modem

_____ _____ _____

Grandma's computer	Kesha's computer

_____ _____

15. Choose the correct words to complete each sentence. You may use a term more than once.

binary code	modem	computer

When signals are sent from a computer, they need to be in

_____. The computer sends the digitized signal to a

_____. This puts the signal on the Internet. The message

first comes to the receiver's _____ before it gets to

their _____.

Sounds in the Air

When you talk on a cell phone, you use radio waves. A cell phone converts your voice (sound waves) into radio waves. These waves then get sent to a cell tower. From here, the waves are relayed to other towers. Finally, a tower sends the radio waves to a receiving phone. This entire process happens almost instantly.

HANDS-ON Apply What You Know

The Phone Is for You!

16. Choose one classmate to be the leader. The leader should write down a message before telling it to the first student. The first student tells the second student the message. The second student tells the third student the story. This is repeated until all the students have heard the message. After the final student has been told, they should say the message aloud. Compare it to what was written down.

HANDS-ON Apply What You Know

Make a Wave

17. Can you use a spring toy to send a message? Using binary code, send a short message to a classmate. "0" is represented by moving the spring back and forth. "1" is represented by moving the spring up and down. Have your classmate say the message aloud. Compare it to what was written down. Are they the same? What might improve your ability to send a message more accurately?

_____

_____

_____

How Cell Phones Help Us Communicate

1

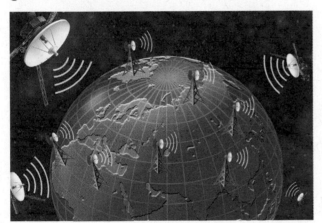

When you talk on a cell phone, the sound waves of your voice are converted into digital code. The code is then sent as radio waves through the air.

2

The sender's radio waves reach cell phone towers, which exist in a network around the world.

3

The waves bounce from tower to tower to satellites and then to other towers.

4

The radio waves are received by a cell phone which converts them back into sound.

18. Choose the correct words to complete each sentence.

sound waves	light wave	radio waves
microwaves	tower	trough

Cells phones convert _____ into _____.

They are then sent to a cell _____. From here, they relay

to other towers. They eventually arrive at a _____ near

another phone.

Bits of Color

Pixels are important. Remember that each picture or image you see on a screen is made of pixels. The more pixels there are, the clearer and more crisp the image will be. Back in the 1980s, videogames and TVs had lower resolution than today. This means that the number of pixels on the screen was smaller. With today's TVs, there are many more pixels. This makes the pictures much clearer and the colors brighter. This is called high resolution, or high definition. You might have heard it called HD.

Does this image really look like an apple? This image has very low resolution. This means there are very few pixels that make it up. The edges look fuzzy. And the texture of the picture looks grainy. This is how television and computer pictures looked many years ago.

Here is an image with higher resolution. Notice how much clearer it is. The image also looks much smoother and more realistic. Most people today like to see high resolution images. This is because they look much more realistic than low resolution.

Putting It Together

19. Choose the correct words to complete each sentence.

light pulses	a system of ones and zeros
Morse	binary

An image on a TV is like the image made in the grid activity because

both rely on _____ to create images. All digital

devices use _____ code to transmit signals.

Discover More

Check out this path . . . or go online to choose one of these other paths.

Elephant Communication

- **People in Science & Engineering**
- **Wave That Flag**

Elephant Stomp Sounds

There are all kinds of sounds. All sound waves have amplitude and wavelength. As humans, we can only hear things that are within a certain wavelength. Some animals can hear sounds that we cannot. Elephants have adapted to generate and hear sounds with longer wavelengths than humans can hear. These sounds are called *infrasounds*. These sounds can travel over great distances. This is very helpful to elephant herds. The sounds can alert them of dangers. They can alert them of a new food source. Being able to hear in this range has been extensively studied in three species of elephants.

Elephants are the largest land animals. Their size makes them fairly safe from predators. They live in large social groups and are constantly "talking" to each other. Most of their sounds are made with their trunks. However, they are able to make rumbling noises from within their bodies. These rumbles cannot be heard by humans.

Elephants may be able to hear through their feet as well as their ears.

219

It has been found that these sounds, called *infrasonic,* are felt by the elephants. They are used as a form of long-distance communication.

Think about where elephants live. Living on the open savannah has many challenges. Infrasonic calls are ideal for living here. Being able to avoid danger is important. Using infrasonic calls lets the elephants stay in touch even if they are not close. Because the signals are heard and felt, scientists believe the elephants take them in through their feet as well as their ears.

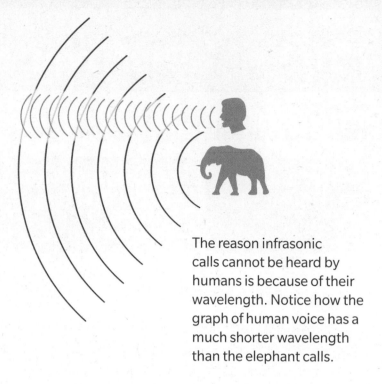

The reason infrasonic calls cannot be heard by humans is because of their wavelength. Notice how the graph of human voice has a much shorter wavelength than the elephant calls.

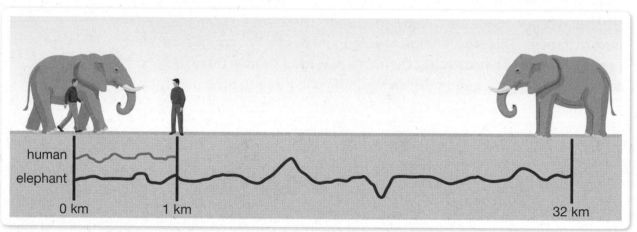

An infrasound made by an elephant can travel large distances. Human speech has shorter wavelengths that don't travel nearly as far.

20. How is the way elephants use infrasonic sounds to communicate alike and different from the way we use cell phones?

_____

_____

_____

_____

_____

_____

Lesson Check

Name _____

Can You Explain It?

1. How has the way we rely on information transfer changed over the years? Be sure to discuss the following:

   • Ways information has been transferred historically.

   • How energy transfer plays a role in information transfer.

   • How information is encoded, moved long distances, and then decoded without losing any of the information.

   • Criteria and constraints of information technology.

> **EVIDENCE NOTEBOOK** Use the information you've collected in your Evidence Notebook to help answer the question.

_____

_____

_____

_____

_____

_____

_____

Checkpoints

2. Which of these methods use technology to transfer information? Select all that apply.

   a. Morse code

   b. using flags

   c. creating a scytale

   d. infrasonic elephant sounds

   e. texting a friend using your phone

3. Suppose you wanted to describe African drums to a classmate. You want to tell them how they are used as a form of sending signals. Which of these would you say? Select all that apply.

   a. The drums send signals you can hear.

   b. The drums have a very high wavelength.

   c. The drums have a very low wavelength.

   d. The drums are used for religious ceremonies.

4. Choose the correct words to complete each of the sentences.

   The ancient Egyptians used _____ as means of story telling and recording their history. Soldiers in ancient China used _____ to send silent messages a long distance. The most famous use of _____ signals was during Paul Revere's ride. The "one if by land, two if by sea" signals told the colonists the British were coming.

   | hieroglyphics |
   | Morse code |
   | drums |
   | smoke signals |
   | lantern |

5. Put these steps in order of how a message would get from your cell phone to your friend's cell phone.

   | tower near your friend's cell phone | tower close to your cell phone | friend's cell phone |

   _____   _____   _____

   | your cell phone | relay |

   _____   _____

6. Use the code key below to decode the message (hint: it is six words long). The message is:

   9 12 5 1 18 14 5 4 13 1 14 25 20 8 9 14 7 19 1 2 15 21 20 19 9 7 14 1 12 19

1	2	3	4	5	6	7	8	9	10	11	12	13
A	B	C	D	E	F	G	H	I	J	K	L	M

14	15	16	17	18	19	20	21	22	23	24	25	26
N	O	P	Q	R	S	T	U	V	W	X	Y	Z

Lesson Roundup

A. Which of these describe the use of hieroglyphics and pictographs in ancient times? Select all that apply.

  a. They were often drawn on walls.

  b. They are a form of signal that can be heard.

  c. They record events and cultural histories.

  d. They were made using modern art tools.

B. How are cell phone signals transferred? Select the best answer for the question.

  a. They go from the tower to the phone to another phone.

  b. They go from the receiver's phone to the sender's phone.

  c. They go from sender to tower to relay to tower to receiver.

  d. They go from tower to receiver to sender to relay back to the receiver.

C. Decide if each phrase is describing signal transfer using coded or uncoded communication. Some may go into more than one category.

Morse code

talking on the phone

coded		uncoded

scytale

text message

talking face to face

D. Why are codes used to relay messages? Select all that apply.

  a. They do not depend on understanding a language.

  b. Everyone can understand them.

  c. They can be encoded and decoded digitally and sent by waves.

  d. They are short.

The Rainbow Show

Your task is to prepare and give a three-part educational presentation about rainbows. In Part One, you'll tell your class all about rainbows, what they are, and how they form. In Part Two, you'll dazzle your class by making a rainbow appear before their eyes. Then in Part Three, you'll wrap it all up by taking your rainbow and sending it back to where it came from.

Rainbows occur all the time in nature. But did you know that you can make your own?

UNDERSTAND YOUR GOAL: Describe a successful "Rainbow Show."

_____

_____

_____

Review the checklist at the end of this Unit Performance Task. Keep those requirements in mind as you proceed.

RESEARCH: Use online and library sources to collect information about rainbows. Find out how rainbows form, what colors they contain, and other facts about them. Consider adding entertainment value to your presentation by finding a short poem about rainbows or some interesting rainbow trivia. Examine several sources, and cite the ones you choose. Describe your findings.

_____

_____

_____

DEMONSTRATION PREPARATION: Use online and library sources to find out how a prism can create a rainbow. Then investigate how a second prism can turn the rainbow's colors back into white light. Describe your findings, and cite your sources.

_____

_____

_____

© Houghton Mifflin Harcourt • Image Credits: ©Goodshoot/Jupiterimages/Getty Images

ARRANGE YOUR INFORMATION: Consider the questions below as you organize and script your show.

1. How can multimedia help you present your information?
2. What information do you want to include?
3. In what order do you want to place your information?
4. What can you add to make your speech entertaining?
5. What materials will you need for your demonstration, and how will you use them?

_____

_____

_____

_____

_____

_____

PREPARE: Script your show. Remember that Part One is for giving information, and Parts Two and Three are for giving demonstrations.

EDITING AND REVISION: Does your planned presentation accomplish the goal that you set for it? Are there ways to improve it? If so, how? Make any changes necessary to improve it.

COMMUNICATE: Present your "Rainbow Show" to your class.

Checklist

Review your project and check off each completed item.

_____ Includes a statement of the presentation's goal.

_____ Includes description of the presentation's content, along with cited sources.

_____ Includes a list of materials needed for the demonstration portions of the presentation.

_____ Includes a script, outlining all three parts of the show.

_____ Includes a hands-on, three-part presentation to the class.

Unit Review

1. What two types of waves are produced by this performance?
   Circle the correct choices.

   a. light waves

   b. water waves

   c. sound waves

   d. seismic waves

2. Which choice names two parts of a wave?
   Circle the correct choice.

   a. size and speed

   b. crest and trough

   c. amplitude and volume

   d. wavelength and reflection

3. Why were Navajo soldiers important during World War II?

   _____

   _____

   _____

   _____

4. Classify each item as an example of back and forth waves (*B*), up and down waves (*U*), or both (*both*).

_____ Music

_____ Light from stars

_____ Satellite signals

_____ Earthquake tremors

5. What qualities is a reflective surface likely to have? Circle all that apply.

   a. It is likely to be shiny.

   b. It is likely to be clear.

   c. It is likely to be dark.

   d. It is likely to be opaque.

6. What sort of object is each recipe box? Write a word from the word bank on each line.

> **transparent   translucent   opaque**

_____

_____

_____

7. Which of these made the telegraph possible? Select all that apply.

   a. the discovery of electricity

   b. the discovery of radio waves

   c. the development of Morse code

   d. the development of flag semaphore

8. Select a word from the word bank to complete the sentence.

pixels scythes bits

A picture looks like a single image, but it is really millions of tiny

dots called _____ .

9. Match the word with its definition.

wavelength   the lowest point of a wave

amplitude   the distance between two crests

volume   the loudness of a sound

crest   the height of a wave

trough   the highest point of a wave

10. Describe how our eyes see. Use the image below to help you.

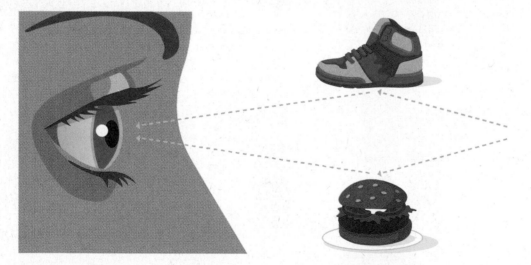

_____

_____

_____

_____

_____

228

Plant Structure and Function

Explore Online

Unit Project: Plant and Animal Partnerships

How does the structure and function of plants and animals work together for pollination? Ask your teacher for details.

Apples are tasty, but they are also vital to the reproduction of apple trees. Plants, like animals, are made of individual structures that serve a specific purpose.

At a Glance

Vocabulary Game: Concentration

Materials
- 1 set of word cards

Setup
- Mix up the cards.
- Place the cards face down on a table in even rows. No card should touch another card.

Directions
1. Take turns to play.
2. Choose two cards. Turn the cards face up.
   - If the cards match, keep the pair and take another turn.
   - If the cards do not match, turn them back over.
3. The game is over when all cards have been matched. The player with the most matched pairs wins.

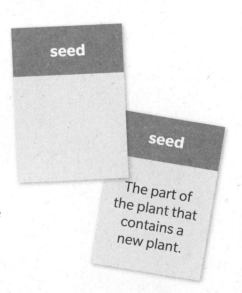

seed

seed

The part of the plant that contains a new plant.

Unit Vocabulary

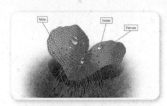

fertilization: The process when male and female reproductive parts join together.

leaf: The part of a plant that makes food using air, light, and water.

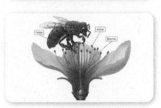

pollination: The transfer of pollen in flowers or cones.

reproduction: To have young, or more living things of the same kind.

root: A plant part that is usually underground and absorbs water and minerals from the soil.

seed: The part of a plant that contains a new plant.

spore: A reproductive structure of some plants, such as mosses and ferns, that can form a new plant.

stem: The part of a plant that holds it up and has tubes that carry water, minerals, and nutrients through the plant.

What Are Some Plant Parts and How Do They Function?

Different plants have different types of structures. The structures function in ways that enable the plants to survive.

By the end of this lesson . . .
you'll be able to identify the different parts of plants and the functions of these parts.

© Houghton Mifflin Harcourt • Image Credit: ©Allstarecho/Wikimedia Commons

Can You Explain It?

Have you ever seen a plant that is bent over to one side? If there are indoor plants in your home or at school, you may have noticed a plant that leans in one direction instead of growing straight up.

1. Why do you think the plants in the pictures bend in the directions that they do? How would this behavior help the plant grow and survive?

_____

_____

_____

_____

_____

_____

_____

_____

 EVIDENCE NOTEBOOK Look for this icon to help you gather evidence to answer the questions above.

Plant Dissection

Do Parts Serve Purposes?

You can tell from a quick glance at a plant that it has different parts. Most plants have certain parts in common that perform the same functions.

Functions of Plant Parts

2. Complete each description then label the plant parts with the correct letter.

| root | stem | leaf | flower |

a. _____ This part of the plant grows down into soil.

b. _____ This part of the plant captures sunlight.

c. _____ This part of the plant grows away from the ground and helps keep the plant upright.

d. _____ This part of the plant attracts insects.

3. Fill in the chart below to explain how you think each of these parts helps a plant survive.

Plant part	How does it help the plant survive?
root	
stem	
leaf	
flower	

Part by Part

Different parts of plants serve different purposes. Read about the functions of these plant parts and how they help the different types of plants survive.

Thorns are sharp, pointed parts on some plants. Thorns protect a plant from being eaten by animals. **Flowers** attract insects and are involved in reproduction so the plant can make new plants.

Cones are involved in the reproduction of certain kinds of plants. **Bark**, a tree's woody covering, protects it from cold temperatures and from animal damage.

Cacti live in dry areas and have **spines** instead of wide, flat leaves. Not having flat leaves reduces water loss. Spines also protect the cactus from animals.

Plants such as ferns and mosses produce **spores**, which are released into the air. When spores land in a spot where conditions are right for growth, a new plant will start to grow.

Roots help hold a plant in place. They also absorb water and nutrients from the soil. These materials are needed for a plant to survive and grow.

Leaves capture sunlight and use it to make food in the form of sugar. Plants use the food to grow. Plant **stems** support leaves and help plants stay upright.

4. How are thorns on a flower and spines on a cactus similar? Select the correct answer.
   a. Both reduce water loss.
   b. Both protect plants from animals.
   c. Both absorb water from soil.
   d. Both hold plants upright.

5. Which function do roots *not* perform?
   a. absorb water from soil
   b. anchor a plant in place
   c. develop seeds for reproduction
   d. absorb nutrients from soil

Similar but Different

When you look around at different plants, you see that they often have the same parts—roots, stems, leaves, flowers, and more. But these parts do not look exactly the same in all plants. Leaves and flowers differ in shape, size, and color. Some plants have thorns. Others do not.

Different Parts, Similar Jobs

6. Compare how the plant parts in each set of photographs function. Write whether the parts most support protection, growth, or reproduction.

A. A **taproot,** can get water from deep underground, and they do well in droughts. They can also store food.

B. **Fibrous roots** can quickly absorb water and nutrients near the soil's surface. They also stop soil erosion.

_____

C. This large, **flat leaf** captures sunlight. Having lots of large leaves in spring and summer helps the plant absorb more sunlight and make more food.

D. The **needles** of evergreens such as pine trees gather sunlight for the plant to make food. Their shape and waxy coating reduce water loss during dry weather.

_____

E. **Woody stems** help plants such as trees and shrubs stay upright in strong winds. They can help trees become very tall. Tall plants get more sunlight.

F. Other plants, such as dandelions and sunflowers, have **green stems.** These stems can also capture sunlight while they hold the plants up and support branches, leaves, and other parts.

_____

G. Plants such as pine trees make **cones** instead of flowers. Male cones release pollen that pollinates female cones. Female cones then hold seeds until they are ready to be released. New plants grow from seeds that land in places with the right conditions.

H. Other types of plants use **spores** to reproduce. Once spores are released, they are carried by wind. If spores land in a place with the right conditions, new plants will grow.

I. Plants such as dandelions and apple trees produce **flowers**. A flower has different parts that are involved in reproduction, including petals and the pollen-producing stamen. Many flowers attract animals that move pollen from one plant to another.

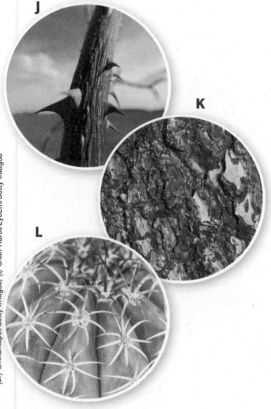

J. Some plants, such as roses, have **thorns** with sharp, pointed ends that can injure an animal that tries to eat the plant.

K. Tough, thick **bark** prevents many animals from eating trees and shrubs. It also helps reduce infections caused by fungi or bacteria getting into a plant.

L. Plants, such as cacti, that live in dry areas have leaves shaped like **spines**. An animal that tries to eat a spiny plant will likely be injured.

Think of the functions of the different plant parts you have learned about. Recall that some plant parts have more than one function. For example, roots absorb water and minerals from the soil, but they also anchor a plant in place.

 EVIDENCE NOTEBOOK Which part of the plant uses light? What does it use light for? Record your explanation in your Evidence Notebook.

 Language SmArts
Writing Opinion Pieces

7. Make a claim about which plant part you think is most important overall for plant growth. Use three facts to provide evidence to support your claim. You may use facts from this lesson. You may also need to do additional research.

Record your claim and your evidence in the table below. Then debate your claim with your classmates.

Claim	Evidence
I think that the _____ is the most important part for plant growth.	Fact 1: _____ _____ _____ _____ _____ Fact 2: _____ _____ _____ _____ _____ Fact 3: _____ _____ _____ _____ _____

What's Inside?

Slurp!

You have already learned that the roots of a plant absorb water and minerals from soil. How does the plant use the water?

Before

Explore Online

You've seen a stalk of celery like this before.

After

If you put a stalk of celery that has been cut in colored water, it will look like this.

8. Why do the leaves become the same color as the colored water? How do you think this happens?

_____

_____

_____

_____

It's What's Inside that Counts

To learn why the celery's appearance changed when it was placed in colored water, take a closer look at the inside of the stems in the two plants below. Each one will show a different system of tubes that helps the plant survive and grow.

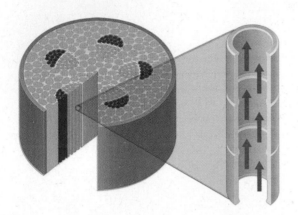

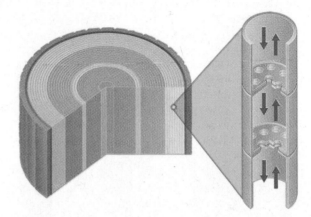

Inside a plant stem is a system of **water-carrying tubes**. Water, taken in from the roots, moves through the tubes into the plant's leaves so the leaves can use the water to make food.

Sugar made in a plant's leaves moves through a system of **food-carrying tubes**. These tubes travel from the leaves, throughout the plant, and down to the roots. Some plant roots, like carrots, store extra sugar produced by the plant.

 9. Language SmArts Briefly describe the two different tube systems in a plant.

_____

_____

_____

_____

_____

10. Write the words in the order in which food moves from one plant part to the next.

roots   tubes   leaves

→   →   stem   →

Green Roofs

Growing grass and plants on the rooftops of buildings in cities helps solve two problems. First, it allows more space to grow plants in cities that have limited space. Second, a grass layer reduces the heating of the building on hot summer days.

In winter, heat from inside the building keeps the grass warmer, which means it can grow for a longer part of the year.

Explore Online

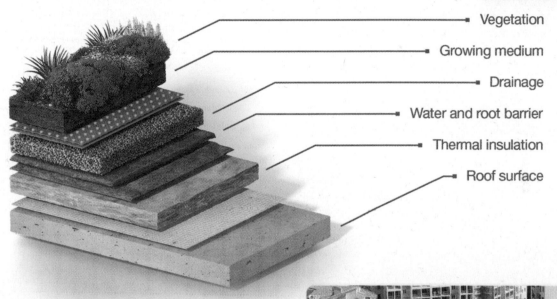

- Vegetation
- Growing medium
- Drainage
- Water and root barrier
- Thermal insulation
- Roof surface

To grow grass on rooftops successfully, you need different layers of materials. To protect the roof and the plants, you need a layer of insulation and then a layer of waterproof material to keep roots from growing into the the roof. Next is a layer of material that will allow water to drain away from the roof. On the top layer are the soil and growing plants.

11. What are some advantages and disadvantages of green roofs? Do additional research if needed.

_____

_____

_____

_____

Modeling Water Flow in Plants

12. Using what you can infer about water moving in celery, make a 3D model of a plant's water system. Your model does not need to function, but do use different arts and crafts materials to represent the different types of materials in the plant.

EVIDENCE NOTEBOOK Think about the tube systems in plants and the leaning plants pictured at the beginning of the lesson. Which tube system needs light to do its function or job?

Putting It Together

13. What color do you see in the celery besides its normal green color? What does this suggest?

_____

_____

14. Use the celery investigation to support the following claim with evidence.

"A celery plant has a tube system that carries water through the plant." Select all evidence statements that apply.

a. I can see the tubes when the celery is cut open.

b. I can see the color of the tubes is the same color as the water when the celery is cut open.

c. The color of water in the bowl got lighter. This means water must have been absorbed by the celery.

d. I can see that the leaves turned the same color as the water.

Hold the Soil

Objective

Collaborate to build a system to grow plants in water instead of soil.

Growing plants in water instead of soil is called hydroponics. As long as plants have the sunlight, space, water, and nutrients they need added to the water, they can grow without soil.

Imagine a company has hired you to grow hydroponic plants. Use your knowledge of plant parts and their functions to design such a system. What will be your goal for the activity?

_____

_____

_____

Materials	Cost
• 5 bean seeds	$3
• plastic cup or bottle	$1 for 1 or $2 for 3
• paper towel	$1 for 2 or $2 for 5
• gravel	$2 per 113 g
• vermiculite	$2 per 113 g
• cotton balls	$1 for 3 or $2 for 10
• foam pellets	$1 per 113 g
• liquid nutrients	$2 per 50 g
• aluminum foil	$1 per ¼ sq. m
• plastic wrap	$1 per ¼ sq. m
• metric ruler	$0
• water	$0

Find a Problem What question will you investigate to meet this objective?

_____

_____

Procedure

STEP 1 Research with your group how to grow seeds in water instead of soil.

STEP 2 Brainstorm ideas for your system in which to grow seeds. Keep the following criteria and constraints in mind.

Criteria	Constraints
☐ Your system should use water in place of soil.	☐ Your system cannot be larger than 30 cm x 15 cm x 15 cm.
☐ Your system should provide the seeds with what they need to sprout and grow.	☐ The total budget for your system must not be greater than $12.

STEP 3 Plan your system. Make a drawing or blueprint on a piece of paper. Draw and label each part of your system.

Explain how you made sure you met the criteria and constraints in your system.

_____

_____

_____

STEP 4 Build your system.

STEP 5 Test your system
Write out the steps.

_____

_____

_____

STEP 6 Observe your system. Record results at least two times a week for four weeks. Use a ruler as a tool to measure the growth of the plants.

Observation Table

Date	Seed/plant growth (cm)	Other observations

Analyze Your Results

STEP 7 How many of your bean seeds sprouted? Of those plants, how many survived four weeks or more? How much did they grow?

_____

_____

_____

STEP 8 Evaluate and Redesign your device. How well did you meet the criteria and constraints? What improvements could you make to your system's design?

_____

_____

_____

Draw Conclusions

STEP 9 Communicate to compare your hydroponic system and results with other groups. Did another group's seeds grow better than yours? Why or why not?

_____

_____

_____

STEP 10 Make a claim based on your investigation. Support your claim with evidence from this activity.

_____

_____

_____

STEP 11 Think of other questions you would like to ask about designing systems to grow plants.

_____

_____

_____

Can Plants Move?

Move and Groove

Have you ever seen a vine grow up the side of a house or wrap around a fence post? What happens if a potted plant gets knocked over on its side and keeps growing? Plants have certain behaviors that help them to grow and survive.

Explore Online

15. In picture **a,** the plant was knocked over on its side and grew in one direction. Why do you think this occurred?

_____

_____

16. In picture **b,** the plant was placed by a window and grew in one direction. Why do you think this occurred?

_____

_____

17. In picture **c,** the leaves of the mimosa folded inward when it was touched. Why do you think this happened?

_____

_____

Oh, Behave!

In nature, plants live in environments where conditions change constantly. The sun is not visible all day. The temperature can change drastically. A herd of animals may rumble through the environment. Whatever the conditions, plants have to absorb sunlight, make food, grow, and survive.

How Do You Grow?

18. Read about plant behaviors below and complete the activity.

Plants **respond to light**. Plants need sunlight to make food, so a house plant that sits in front of a window will grow toward the light. If the plant is not turned regularly, it will become very lopsided. Circle the image that shows what will happen if this plant is left in the window.

The roots of plants grow down toward the center of Earth in **response to gravity**. The stem of a plant grows in the opposite direction, away from the center of Earth. This usually results in the stem growing upward. Circle the image that shows what will happen if this plant is knocked over.

Some plants respond to touch. A leaf might curl up to protect a plant from damage or from being eaten. A Venus flytrap clasps its leaves closed if an insect touches the fine hairs on the inside of the leaves. For plants that eat insects, this is an important **response to touch**. Circle the image that shows what will happen when the fly lands on the leaf.

247

EVIDENCE NOTEBOOK Which photo on the previous page shows a plant's bending behavior similar to what you saw at the beginning of the lesson? Describe the similarities in your Evidence Notebook.

HANDS-ON Apply What You Know

Plant Response

19. Choose one of the ways a plant responds to its environment. Draw a comic strip with at least three panels showing one of the plant behaviors you learned about. Write captions for each panel you draw.

_____ _____ _____

_____ _____ _____

_____ _____ _____

_____ _____ _____

Language SmArts
Multiple Sources

20. Using multiple sources, explain how plant behavior helps plants survive. Cite your sources.

_____

_____

_____

_____

_____

Tip

The English Language Arts Handbook can provide help with understanding how to use and cite multiple sources.

Discover More

Check out this path . . . or go online to choose one of these other paths.

People in Science & Engineering

- Burrr!
- How Unusual!

Clayton Anderson

Explore Online

Clayton Anderson is an engineer and an astronaut. Aboard the International Space Station, he worked with growth chambers containing tiny plants to observe how plants grow in space. Remember that aboard a space station, a plant's environment is very different from on Earth, so the plant might respond differently.

While there is gravity in space, people and things on the space station experience it differently than we do on Earth. Everything appears to be floating. Think about how this affects plants in ways such as keeping soil in a container or watering a plant. It takes some problem solving to sprout seeds in space.

When a plant grows on Earth, its stem grows away from Earth while its roots grow toward Earth. If a potted plant is knocked onto its side, the sideways stem will grow up at an angle, and the roots will grow down.

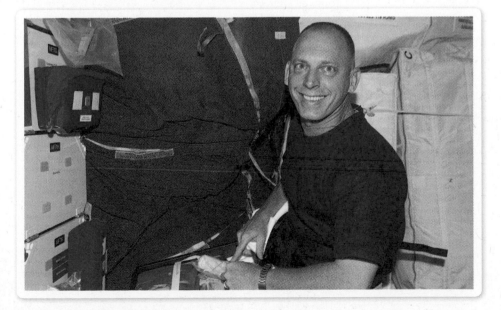

Clayton Anderson, engineer and astronaut

© Houghton Mifflin Harcourt • Image Credits: ©Design Pics Inc./Alamy

Engineer It!
Upside Down Plants

21. Suppose you are a scientist who has been hired by a science museum. Your job is to make a device to hang a plant upside down to teach young children about how plants respond to the force of gravity.

Procedure

A. Find a Problem to solve.

_____

_____

B. Brainstorm ideas with your team on how to build your device. Keep in mind the following criteria and constraints:

Criteria	Constraints
☐ The device must cause the plant to hang upside down.	☐ Not including the plant and soil, you can only use five materials to build it.
☐ The stem and the roots must be able to grow out of the device.	☐ The device must be made of 50% recycled materials
☐ Minimal soil should fall from the device when it hangs upside down.	

C. Plan your device. Make a drawing. Then, have your teacher approve your design, including whatever equipment may be needed to hang the device.

D. Build your device.

E. Test your device by placing soil and a plant in it. Observe the plant's response over time to being flipped upside down, and keep data about your observations.

F. Evaluate and Redesign your device. How did you meet the criteria and constraints? How could you improve your device?

_____

_____

_____

_____

G. Communicate your findings with your classmates. Compare and contrast the results.

Lesson Check

Name _____

Can You Explain It?

1. Now that you've learned more about plant parts and the functions they perform, explain why a plant bends as its light source moves. Be sure to do the following:

   • Explain the relationship between sunlight and food in plants.

   • Identify the role of each plant part in capturing and using sunlight.

   • Describe how growth and food relate to better chances of survival for a plant.

EVIDENCE NOTEBOOK Use the information you've collected in your Evidence Notebook to help you cover each point above.

_____

_____

_____

_____

_____

_____

_____

_____

Checkpoints

2. Which parts of a plant help protect it from animals? Select all that apply.
   a. bark
   b. leaves
   c. spines
   d. thorns

3. Study the parts of the image. Write the letter of the correct label for the material that is carried by the system of tubes in each image. All labels may not apply.

    a. food

    b. soil

    c. water

    d. heat

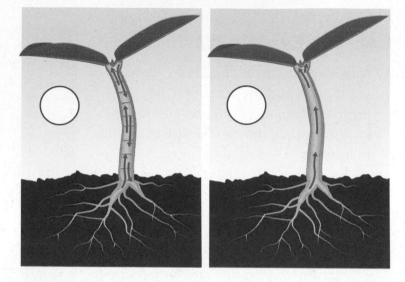

4. Support this claim with the correct evidence below: Roots help plants grow.

    a. Roots absorb water, which plants need to make food.

    b. Roots capture sunlight, which gives plants a source of energy for making food.

    c. Roots help protect plants from animals.

    d. Roots help plants reproduce.

5. Which answer correctly states how the food system in a plant functions?

    a. Leaves absorb water, which plants need to make food.

    b. leaves produce food using sunlight, food moves down the tubes to the rest of the plant

    c. roots absorb nutrients, nutrients move up the tubes and turn to sugar

6. Plants respond to _____ when they make food. Some plants respond to _____ when they trap food. In response to _____, plant parts bend so each part is in the right position to do its special job.

| gravity |
| light |
| touch |

Lesson Roundup

A. Write the main function of each plant part.

| growth | reproduction | protection |

Stem _____

Roots _____

Flower _____

Spines _____

B. Choose all the correct descriptions about plant tube systems.

   a. Water moves from the roots of a plant to the rest of the plant through a system of tubes.

   b. Food moves from the roots of a plant to the rest of the plant through a system of leaves.

   c. Food moves from the leaves of a plant to the rest of the plant through a system of tubes.

   d. Water moves from the leaves of a plant to the rest of the plant through a system of tubes.

C. Write the letter of the type of response that each picture shows.

| **a.** response to touch |
| **b.** response to gravity |
| **c.** response to light |

How Do Plants Grow and Reproduce?

As with animals, plants also grow and reproduce. Whether the plant is a tree, a kind of grass, or a flower, it begins its life as a seed. Under the right conditions, the seeds in this picture will grow into different kinds of plants.

By the end of this lesson . . .
you'll be able to explain how plants grow and reproduce.

Can You Explain It?

▷ Explore Online

Madison was excited about a fruit tree in the backyard of her new home. As spring began, she observed the tree every day, and noticed several bees near the tree.

A couple of months later, Madison noticed some of the flowers started to swell, while others began to wither and turn brown. She wondered what was happening.

Gradually the bulges left over from the flowers got bigger. Slowly but surely the fruit grew and grew. Eventually, the tree was covered in ripe apples.

1. How did the one flower turn into fruit? Why did some of the other flowers not turn into fruit?

Tip

To recall the names of many parts of plants, read What Are Some Plant Parts and How Do They Function?

_____

_____

_____

_____

_____

_____

_____

_____

_____

 EVIDENCE NOTEBOOK Look for this icon to help you gather evidence to answer the questions above.

Why Do Plants Have Flowers?

Flower Power

Have you ever looked closely at a flower? There are structures inside a flower that help the plant reproduce. View the illustration below to learn more about the names and functions of these structures.

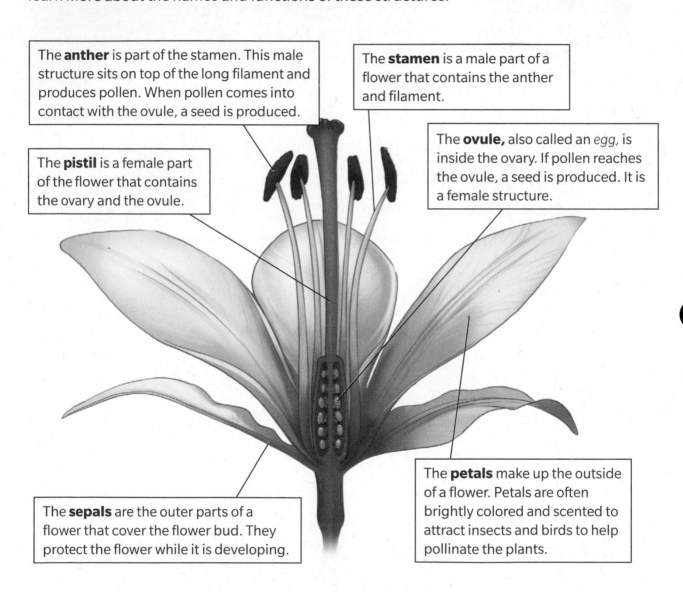

The **anther** is part of the stamen. This male structure sits on top of the long filament and produces pollen. When pollen comes into contact with the ovule, a seed is produced.

The **stamen** is a male part of a flower that contains the anther and filament.

The **pistil** is a female part of the flower that contains the ovary and the ovule.

The **ovule,** also called an *egg,* is inside the ovary. If pollen reaches the ovule, a seed is produced. It is a female structure.

The **sepals** are the outer parts of a flower that cover the flower bud. They protect the flower while it is developing.

The **petals** make up the outside of a flower. Petals are often brightly colored and scented to attract insects and birds to help pollinate the plants.

2. Choose the correct words from the diagram that complete the sentences.

The _____ cover and protect the flower bud. The _____ is where

pollen is produced. If pollen comes into contact with the _____, a

seed is produced.

256

Where Did the Pollen Go?

You know that flowers produce pollen. You have likely seen yellow dust floating in the air or coating the top of a car during the spring or summer. This is pollen. If you are allergic to pollen, you know exactly when flowers are producing it in high amounts! Pollen is necessary for the reproduction of flowering plants.

Explore Online

Pollination is the transfer of pollen from one flower to another. Animals, like hummingbirds, are attracted to the flowers to feed on their sweet, sugary nectar. As an animal, like this hummingbird, feeds on the nectar, some of the pollen sticks to its body.

After the hummingbird moved to the next flower to feed, some of the pollen on its body fell off onto the new flower. The pollen grew a tube down to the ovule and fertilization occurred. **Fertilization** is the process when male and female reproductive parts join together.

 3. Language SmArts Summarize the process a flowering plant goes through for fertilization using the words *pollination* and *fertilization*.

_____

_____

_____

_____

_____

_____

Reproduction is when a plant makes new plants. When pollen reaches an ovule, a seed begins to develop. Eventually, the seed will be moved from the flower to a new location. If the new location has the right conditions, the seed will grow into a new plant. This means that the original plant has reproduced.

In More Ways than One

You've already read about one way that pollen can be moved from one plant to another with help from birds. View the images to learn other ways pollination can take place.

Some plants are pollinated by animals called pollinators. These animals are attracted to the nectar by the sweet smell of the flower. When they eat, pollen sticks to their faces or bodies. As they move from one flower to another, the pollen is also transferred.

Unlike most sweet-smelling flowers, the skunk cabbage in this photo smells like rotting meat. This stinky plant attracts flies. The flies land on the flowers, get pollen on their bodies, and move pollen from flower to flower as they fly around.

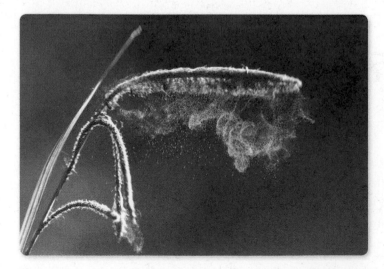

Some plants do not depend on animals for pollination. Instead, their pollen is moved by the wind. This plant releases pollen that drifts in the wind. If the pollen lands on the same type of plant, fertilization can occur.

Some flowers can self-pollinate. This means that the pollen made by the anther is the same pollen that fertilizes the ovule. The pollen does not come from another plant.

4. Which choices are ways pollen can move from one flower to another? Select all that apply.

a. insects **b.** birds **c.** rain **d.** wind

EVIDENCE NOTEBOOK Now that you've learned how pollination occurs, think about the image from the beginning of the lesson. What pollinators did you see? What were they doing to the flower? How does the flower change as a result of their visit?

HANDS-ON Apply What You Know

Pollination Models

5. Make two models of flowers using cups to represent the flowers. Place a cotton ball in each to represent the stamen. Sprinkle some powder on one of the cotton balls to represent pollen. Using a pipe cleaner to represent a bee's leg, how can you model moving pollen from one flower to the other? Try it!

How did you model pollination? What is another way you could model pollination using these materials?

_____

_____

_____

_____

6. You have now learned the steps of pollination and fertilization. Describe what is happening in each image, and number the images in the correct order.

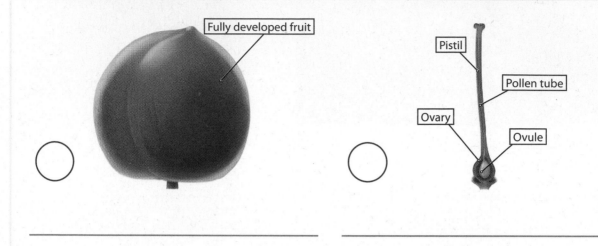

Fully developed fruit

Pistil

Pollen tube

Ovary

Ovule

○

○

_____

_____

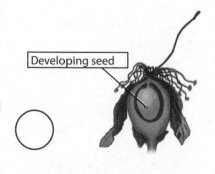

Developing seed

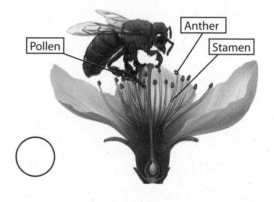

Pollen

Anther

Stamen

○

○

_____

_____

_____

_____

Putting It Together

7. Look at the photos above. How do all these parts involved in reproduction form a system? What would happen if one or more parts of the system wasn't doing its job?

_____

_____

_____

What If Plants Don't Produce Flowers?

Flowerless

Not all plants produce flowers. The fern and the pine tree shown in the images are examples of plants that do not produce flowers. They have different ways to reproduce.

A fern has spores.

A pine tree has cones.

8. How do you think plants reproduce without flowers?

_____

_____

_____

HANDS-ON Apply What You Know

Pinecone Parts

9. Get a pinecone from your teacher, and put it on a paper plate. Explore the pinecone to see its different structures. Draw what you see in detail. Dissect some of the seeds, and draw the structures you see inside. Is the pinecone male or female? What evidence do you see to support your decision?

_____

_____

_____

Ladies and Gentlemen

The pine tree you just saw does not produce flowers to reproduce. Instead, it produces cones. View the timeline to learn more about how pine trees and other trees like it, such as fir trees, reproduce.

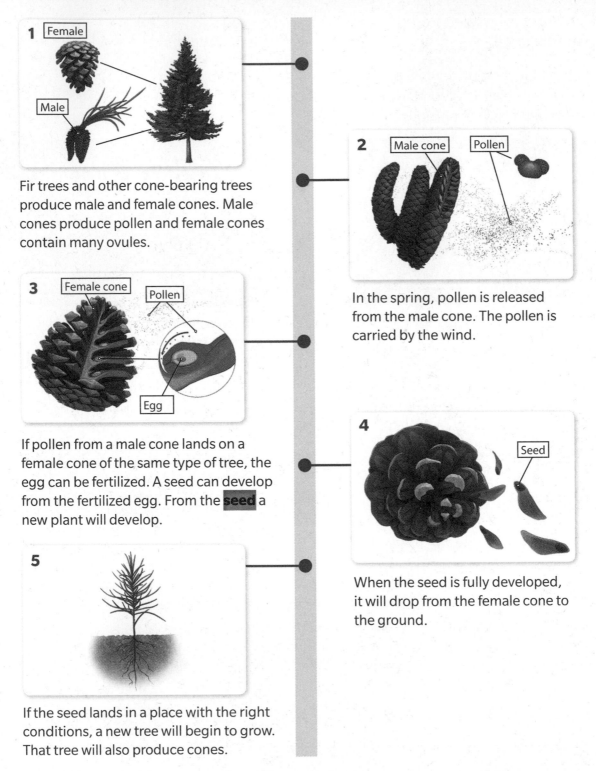

1 Female / Male

Fir trees and other cone-bearing trees produce male and female cones. Male cones produce pollen and female cones contain many ovules.

2 Male cone / Pollen

In the spring, pollen is released from the male cone. The pollen is carried by the wind.

3 Female cone / Pollen / Egg

If pollen from a male cone lands on a female cone of the same type of tree, the egg can be fertilized. A seed can develop from the fertilized egg. From the **seed** a new plant will develop.

4 Seed

When the seed is fully developed, it will drop from the female cone to the ground.

5

If the seed lands in a place with the right conditions, a new tree will begin to grow. That tree will also produce cones.

10. Which structure, or part, of a fir tree holds the pollen needed for reproduction?

a. the female cone   **b.** the male cone   **c.** the male and female cones

How Unique!

Besides cones, there is another way that plants reproduce. They produce spores, which fall to the ground or are carried on the wind. **Spores** are the reproductive part of certain types of plants. If they land in a place where conditions are right, a new plant will begin to grow. View the timeline to learn more about this type of reproduction in plants.

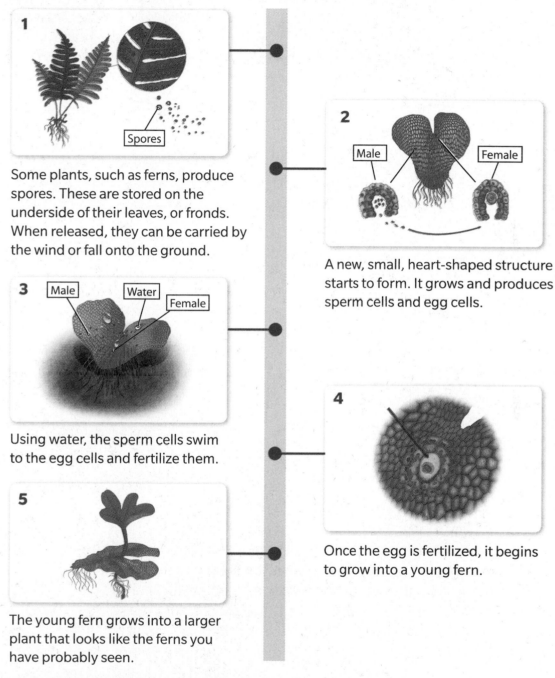

1 Spores

Some plants, such as ferns, produce spores. These are stored on the underside of their leaves, or fronds. When released, they can be carried by the wind or fall onto the ground.

2 Male   Female

A new, small, heart-shaped structure starts to form. It grows and produces sperm cells and egg cells.

3 Male   Water   Female

Using water, the sperm cells swim to the egg cells and fertilize them.

4

Once the egg is fertilized, it begins to grow into a young fern.

5

The young fern grows into a larger plant that looks like the ferns you have probably seen.

11. Choose the correct answer. What is the function of a spore?

    a. Spores fertilize eggs, which then make new ferns.

    b. Spores become structures that produce sperm cells and eggs.

    c. Spores fertilize sperm cells, which then make new ferns.

12. Look at the pictures of plants at the top of the chart, and compare them. Put a check mark for each true statement about the plant.

Uses insects to pollinate			
Produces a seed			
Produces a spore			
Produces a cone			
Has male and female structures			

 EVIDENCE NOTEBOOK What type of reproductive method and structure did Madison's apple tree have? What evidence supports your answer?

 Language SmArts
Using Evidence

13. A man wants to plant a garden with a few plants and let them reproduce to fill up his backyard. He lives in an environment that gets very little rain and is very windy at times. There are some birds but not many flying insects. Based on the scenario, Chantelle thinks plants that reproduce with spores would do well here but flowers and cones would not. Do you agree or disagree? Support your answer with evidence. Write your answers on the lines below. Then debate with your classmates.

_____

_____

_____

_____

On The Move

How Do Seeds Get Around?

When plants release seeds, it is best for the seeds to be moved away from the parent plant. Seeds cannot move on their own, so how do they get around? Some of the ways are the same ways that pollen gets moved from one flower to another.

Agents of Dispersal

14. Look at the three photos on the top row. Each of these structures either contains seeds or is a seed. Match the photo by drawing a line to the photo on the bottom row that shows how each seed is moved from one place to another.

15. Why is it important for seeds to spread out?

_____

_____

_____

Seed Dispersal

When seeds spread out, it helps prevent overcrowding and competition for space, light, and other resources. Read to find out more about how seeds move.

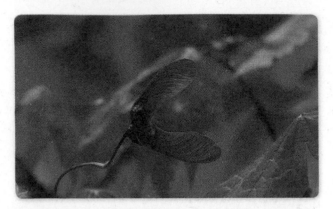

The sycamore tree produces a seed that is sometimes called a helicopter seed, due to its winged shape. The seeds spin as the wind carries them away from the tree and onto the ground.

Some animals eat berries from trees. The fruits contain seeds, like the seed you find in the middle of an apple. After the fruit passes through an animal's digestive tract, the seeds are released in the animal's droppings elsewhere.

Some seeds have tiny hairs or bristles that cause them to stick to peoples' clothes or animals' fur when they brush up against the seeds. The seeds are then carried to a new location by the person or animal.

Some plants depend on water to move their seeds. Some seeds, including the coconut shown here, are light in weight and float in water. When the seeds are dropped in the water, they float to a new spot.

Some plants have a unique way of dispersing seeds. The seeds explode out of the seedpod and fly through the air. Seeds may fly several feet from the parent plant through this method.

16. Which methods can carry seeds far from the parent plant?

    a. animals   **b.** water   **c.** wind

EVIDENCE NOTEBOOK You learned that apples grow from flowers. Construct an argument to prove that apples grow on apple trees as part of the tree's life cycle. Present the apple tree as a system. Identify the parts of the system and how they change during the life of the tree. Record your argument in your Evidence Notebook.

Language SmArts
Inference

You have read about several ways that seeds are dispersed. Answer the questions below to test your understanding.

17. The seeds of a milkweed plant are very light and have fluffy white hairs around them, similar to a dandelion seed. How do you think these seeds are dispersed? Explain your reasoning.

_____

_____

_____

18. Explain how a deer eating a ripe tomato out of a garden might lead to the tomato plant's seeds being moved from one place to another.

_____

_____

_____

© Houghton Mifflin Harcourt • Image Credits: ©Irwin Barrett/First Light/Getty Images

Tip

The English Language Arts Handbook can provide help with understanding how to summarize.

Flying High

Objective

Collaborate Design and test a device that disperses a seed using wind.

A company has hired you to build a device to disperse a seed using wind. Use your knowledge of how seeds are dispersed by wind to design the device.

Find a Problem: What question will you investigate to meet this objective?

_____

_____

Materials
- corn kernels for seeds $3
- balloons $1 for 1 or
                                  $2 for 3
- tissues $1 for 2
                                  $2 for 5
- paper clips $1 for 5
- rubber bands $2 for 2
- straws $1 for 3
- paper bag $1 for 2
- yarn $2 per m
- ribbon $1 per m
- aluminum foil $1 per ¼ sq. m
- tape $1 per roll
- cotton balls $1 for 2
- craft sticks $1 for 2
- pipe cleaners $1 for 2
- fan $0
- meterstick $0

Procedure

STEP 1 Research with your group to find more information about how seeds are dispersed by wind.

STEP 2 Brainstorm ideas for your device. Keep in mind the criteria and constraints below.

Criteria	Constraints
☐ Seed should travel by wind.	☐ Do not use the force of your hand to propel the seed forward.
☐ When device lands, seed should make contact with the ground to reproduce.	☐ Seed must travel at least 30 cm through the air.
	☐ Total budget is $10.

What method of seed dispersal will your device model?

_____

_____

STEP 3 **Plan** by making a drawing of your device. Write out the steps of your experiment to test your device.

_____

_____

_____

_____

_____

_____

_____

_____

STEP 4 Show your drawing and procedure to your teacher. Make any improvements suggested by your teacher. Have your teacher approve your final device and procedure.

STEP 5 **Build** a prototype of your device using the materials you selected.

STEP 6 **Test** your device. Carry out your experiment, and record your results.

Record your results in the observation table.

Trial	Distance seed traveled (cm)	Other observations:
1		
2		
3		
4		

Analyze Your Results

STEP 7 **Evaluate** your test. What was the normal distance your seeds traveled? Do you think they could travel farther if you improved your device? Explain how you would improve your device.

_____

_____

_____

STEP 8 **Redesign** your device. What improvements could you make to your design? If time allows, redesign and retest your device.

_____

_____

_____

STEP 9 **Communicate** to compare your device to other groups' devices and their results. Did their seeds travel farther than yours? Why or why not?

_____

_____

_____

Draw Conclusions

STEP 10 Make a claim based on your investigation. Cite evidence from your design and other designs to support your claim.

_____

_____

_____

STEP 11 Think of other questions you would like to ask about seed dispersal.

_____

_____

_____

Discover More

Check out this path . . . or go online to choose one of these other paths.

Careers in
Science &
Engineering

- **Wait, There's More!**
- **It's What's on the Inside**

Pomologist

The science of growing fruit is known as *pomology*. Scientists who study how to grow fruits are known as *pomologists*.

Dr Janine Hasey is a pomologist and master gardener who specializes in finding better ways to grow fruits and nuts, such as kiwi and walnuts. Pomologists also perform tests to grow larger, better tasting fruits.

One thing that is essential to growing fruit is having a flower pollinated. In certain plants, after a flower is pollinated, it produces a fruit around the seeds. The fruit helps protect the seeds and also helps with seed dispersal.

Dr. Hasey researches ways to control pests and diseases that harm fruits and nuts. She studies the difference between animals that are pollinators and animals that are pests.

19. What does a pomologist do?

_____

_____

_____

_____

_____

Pollinator Project

20. In this activity, you will research three or four pollinators. Make a booklet of your findings. Include a drawing or photo of the pollinator, the type of plants it pollinates, and its importance to the reproduction of plants. Then, compare them below. Submit your booklet to your teacher.

Comparing and Contrasting

Similarities	Differences
_____	_____
_____	_____
_____	_____
_____	_____
_____	_____
_____	_____
_____	_____
_____	_____

21. Which pollinators were similar? What did they have in common?

_____

_____

_____

22. Compare and contrast your findings with your classmates. What similarities and differences did you observe?

_____

_____

_____

Lesson Check

Name _____

Can You Explain It?

1. Look back at the images from the beginning of the lesson. Think about what you have learned about plant reproduction.

• Explain how plants develop from seeds to a fully grown plant.

• Explain the difference between flowering and nonflowering plants.

• Describe how seeds spread out and why.

Explore Online

EVIDENCE NOTEBOOK Use the information you've collected in your Evidence Notebook to help you cover each point above.

_____

_____

_____

_____

_____

_____

_____

Checkpoints

2. Plant parts work together as a system for reproduction. Number the steps of the system in the correct order.

_____ The seed develops and drops to the ground .

_____ The egg is fertilized.

_____ A new tree can begin to grow.

_____ It lands on the female cone.

_____ Pollen is released by the male cone.

Choose the correct answer.

3. How does the pine tree in the picture reproduce?

    a. by producing flowers

    b. by producing cones

    c. by producing spores

4. Which plant structures are used in reproduction? Circle all that apply.

    a. leaves

    b. spores

    c. flowers

    d. wind

    e. cones

5. Read the evidence below, and then choose the best claim.

    • Wind blows pollen.

    • Flies can pollinate plants.

    • Some plants use cones to reproduce.

    • Spores produce egg and sperm cells.

    a. Pollinators are the best way to pollinate plants.

    b. There are many ways for plants to reproduce.

    c. Water is the quickest way for seeds to move.

    d. Spores use wind to reproduce.

6. Write the correct words to complete the sentences.

an animal	**wind**	**water**	**burst from**
stay inside	**flowers**	**fruits**	

If a plant produces seeds that are sticky or bristled, _____

most likely moves the seeds from one place to another. Some plants

have seeds that _____ a seedpod as a way of seed

dispersal. A dandelion produces light, fluffy seeds that are carried by

_____. Birds, bats, and monkeys are examples of animals

that eat the _____ of plants and disperse seeds in their

droppings.

Lesson Roundup

A. Match each flower part to its description by filling in the blank.

| stamen anther pollen pistil ovary ovule |

a. _____ the part of a flower that contains the anther

b. _____ part of the flower where pollen is produced

c. _____ When this comes into contact with the ovule, a seed is produced.

d. _____ the part of the flower that contains the ovary

e. _____ contains the ovule

f. _____ If pollen reaches this structure, a seed is produced.

B. Study the illustrations below. Match each plant to the description of how it reproduces.

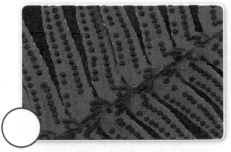

a. This plant produces spores that, if they land in the right place, grow into a heart-shaped structure. This structure grows and produces sperm cells and egg cells.

b. This plant produces cones. In the spring, pollen is released from the male cone. If pollen from a male cone lands on a female cone of the same type of tree, the egg will be fertilized.

C. Choose the correct answer.

A plant produces berries that have seeds inside them. What is the most likely way that the seeds are moved from one place to another?

    a. wind   **b.** water   **c.** animals

A plant produces fruit or seeds that float. Which is the most likely way its seeds are moved from one place to another?

    a. wind   **b.** water   **c.** animals

Flower Parts

You work for a nursery that is putting together a botanist's handbook. Your team is tasked with making an educational illustration of a specific flower. To do that, you'll need to dissect the flower and identify its individual parts. Then you'll need to draw those parts separately and write a caption for each that names it and explains its function.

A flower has many parts, and each has a function of its own.

DEFINE YOUR TASK: What will your completed assignment look like?

_____

_____

_____

Before beginning, review the checklist at the end of this Unit Performance Task. Keep those items in mind as you proceed.

RESEARCH: For this project, your teacher will play the role of your company's Project Coordinator, assigning your team its flower. Your team will be the only one in class with your specific flower. Use online or library resources to identify your flower and learn its parts. Cite your sources.

_____

_____

MAKE A PLAN: Consider the questions below as you plan your procedure for dissecting your flower and examining, illustrating, and describing its parts.

1. What tools and equipment will we need to dissect our flower?

_____

_____

2. What parts will we look for as we dissect our flower?

_____

_____

3. What materials will we need to make our illustrations?

_____

_____

_____

These students are looking closely at the different parts of a flower.

4. How large should we make our illustrations and how thoroughly should we describe the parts of our flower?

_____

_____

_____

5. How should we arrange our illustrations? Should we include one illustration of the complete flower?

_____

_____

_____

DISSECT AND ILLUSTRATE: Dissect your flower. Draw, label, and describe each part of your illustrations as described in your plan.

COMMUNICATE: Give a short presentation to your class about your team's flower, what you learned from dissecting it, and what your team's illustrations teach the viewer. If there is time, the entire class can discuss similarities and differences among their different assigned flowers.

☑ Checklist

Review your project and check off each completed item.

_____ All questions on the page are answered.

_____ Includes an educational illustration of the parts of your team's flower.

_____ Includes a demonstration and oral report about your team's procedures and illustration.

Unit Review

1. Support this claim with evidence: A leaf's function is to make food for the plant.

2. Which two structures serve an identical function in plants? Circle both.

 a. roots
 b. stems
 c. flowers
 d. spores
 e. spines

3. Explain in detail how the food and water tubes work with other plant parts such as roots, stems, and leaves to provide a system.

© Houghton Mifflin Harcourt

278

4. Place each term under the word that describes what it does. Some boxes have more than one word.

| roots | spore | bark | leaf | thorn |

Growth	Protection	Reproduction

5. Complete the sentences using the words in the word bank.

| bark | roots | spines | leaves | thorns |

Some trees and shrubs have thick _____ to protect them

from animals. _____, along with _____,

protect other plants by injuring animals that eat them.

6. Which of the following must combine for a seed to form? Circle all that apply.

   a. bark

   b. roots

   c. pollen

   d. ovule

   e. thorns

7. The pine tree is an example of a plant that reproduces

using _____ instead of flowers.

   a. flowers

   b. cones

   c. spores

   d. ferns

8. Using the numbers 1–5, place the steps that led to the development of the fruit shown here.

_____ Flowers appeared.

_____ The oranges appeared.

_____ Buds appeared on the tree.

_____ Some of the flowers began to swell.

_____ Insects and birds began to visit the tree.

9. What are some behavior responses plants have? Circle all that apply.

   a. respond to light

   b. respond to touch

   c. respond to smells

   d. respond to gravity

10. Complete the sentences using the words in the word bank.

> **spores**   **flowers**   **male and female**   **animal**

Ferns produce _____ instead of seeds. All plants

reproduce using _____ cells.

Animal Structure and Function

Explore Online

Unit Project: Chew Clue
How can you identify an animal based on its teeth? You will conduct an investigation with your team. Ask your teacher for details.

Skin is an important organ many animals have to protect their internal parts from outside dangers. Skin can be soft like on human eyelids, or very hard, like these plates on the rhinoceros.

At a Glance

Vocabulary Game: Concentration

Materials
- 1 set of word cards

Setup
- Mix up the cards.
- Place the cards face down on a table in even rows. No card should touch another card.

Directions
1. Take turns to play.

2. Choose two cards. Turn the cards face up.
   - If the cards match, keep the pair and take another turn.
   - If the cards do not match, turn them back over.

3. The game is over when all cards have been matched. The player with the most matched pairs wins.

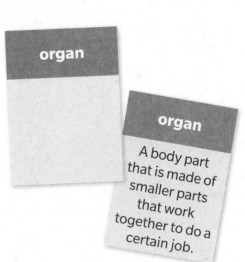

organ

organ

A body part that is made of smaller parts that work together to do a certain job.

Unit Vocabulary

external structures: Those parts on the outside of a body or structure.

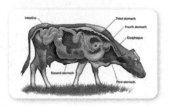

internal structures: Those parts on the inside of a body or structure.

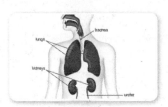

organ: A body part that is made of smaller parts that work together to do a certain job.

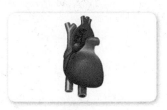

organ system: A group of organs that work together to do a job for the body.

receptors: Special structures that send information about the environment from different parts of the body to the brain.

What Are Some External Structures of Animals?

Animals come in all different shapes and sizes. They move around in different ways, too. What kinds of parts does this starfish have for moving? How does it use those parts to accomplish what it needs to do?

By the end of this lesson . . .
you'll identify how external animal structures serve functions in growth, survival, behavior, and reproduction.

Can You Explain It?

Lizards are excellent climbers, expertly moving around. Most lizards climb like the one on the left. The lizard on the red wall on the right is called a gecko. How are its feet different from the other lizard?

1. What did you observe about the two lizards in the photos? You can see how the lizard on the left is moving on the grass. But how is the surface the gecko is climbing different from the grass? How do you think the gecko's external structures are different?

_____

_____

_____

_____

_____

_____

_____

EVIDENCE NOTEBOOK Look for this icon to help you gather evidence to answer the question above.

Body Building

It's All in the Skin

Animals that live in different environments have to deal with different conditions. These conditions can limit or control what characteristics animals that live in those environments can have to survive.

Body Coverings

2. Match each description with the animal covering it describes.

a. Moisture and oxygen passes easily through the thin, moist skin. The animal needs to live in a wet and warm environment.

c. A slimy substance produced by the skin keeps it from drying out in the warm environment.

b. Thick hairs trap heat produced by the animal's body to keep the animal warm in cold environments.

d. Transparent, hollow hairs of the fur appear white so the animal can blend into its environment.

Animals have **external structures** that allow them to live, grow, reproduce, and survive. External structures are structures on the outside of an organism. The external structures of the frog wouldn't allow it to survive in the Arctic, but it can survive in a warmer, wetter environment.

A polar bear has external structures meant for an Arctic environment. Take a look at the polar bear picture again, and describe what you think an Arctic environment is like and how a polar bear would survive there.

 EVIDENCE NOTEBOOK Animals have many external structures that function to support survival, growth, behavior, and reproduction. Make a list of some of the other structures you see in the photos above.

Moving Parts

3. Animals have structures that help them move. Look at the pictures below and record similarities and differences. Think about the way these animals move.

Explore Online

An ant crawls along with its six legs.

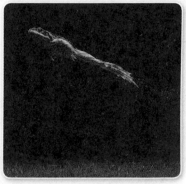

The two, larger hind legs of the frog are strong, allowing it to jump far.

Alike:

Different:

A bat's wings are thin, stretchy membranes made of skin that catch the air to fly.

A pigeon flaps its feathered wings to move it up in the air.

Alike:

Different:

The tail of the shark pushes from side to side against the water, moving it along.

A dolphin pushes its tail up and down to move forward in the water.

Alike:

Different:

287

Moving Through the Environment

Animals are adapted, or fit well, to the environments in which they live. They have external body parts that help them move about on land, in the air, or through the water.

Land, Water, or Air?

4. Based on your observations of the external structures of these animals, label whether the animal best moves on land, in air, or in water.

_____ _____ _____

Although most animals have structures for moving in their environment, there are some animals that don't often move from place to place. Corals, sponges, and barnacles are animals that mostly stay in one place. These animals have structures that let them catch food even though they cannot move.

 5. Language SmArts What do the animals moving about in each environment have in common? List similarities in structures you observe in the animals.

_____

_____

_____

_____

_____

Time to Eat

Animals have external structures that they use to eat. Look at the photos to see how they get food.

▶ Explore Online

Mountain lions have powerful jaws with very sharp teeth inside their mouths.

Antelopes have mouths with flat teeth at the front. This allows them to bite grass close to the ground.

Giant tubeworms have no mouths! Instead of eating, they get nutrients from tiny organisms that live in them.

Eagles have very large, hooked beaks that easily tear apart flesh.

The frog has a flexible jaw that allows it to open wide to snatch food and a long sticky tongue.

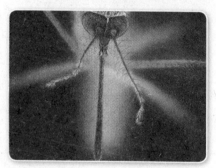

The female mosquito uses its tube-like mouth part to pierce skin and suck blood.

6. What do you think these animals eat, based on the structures of their mouth parts? What inferences can you make?

Animal	What does it eat?	What's your evidence?
mountain lion		
antelope		
female mosquito		
golden eagle		
frog		
giant tubeworm		

Take Cover

Animals can be soft, hard, rough, slimy, or have spines. There are many kinds of coverings that protect the insides of an animal's body.

▷ **Explore Online**

Fur helps insulate this alpaca, preventing heat loss in the cold mountains.

Birds have feathers to keep warm. They are also necessary for the bird to fly.

A snake's smooth scales help it grip and push against surfaces to move.

A hard shell covers some animals, such as tortoises, for protection.

Some animals have sharp spines on their skin to keep them safe.

A sea cucumber's leathery skin protects it from predators.

What's the Purpose?

7. Select the best answer from the word bank that describes each animal covering and completes the sentence.

> predators   body   scales   shells   spines

_____ cover the length of the fish's _____.

A sea urchin has _____ for protection from _____.

feathers	fur	cool	warm	breathe
breathe	fat	wet	moist	flight

Guinea pigs are covered with _____. This helps keep them _____.

A blue jay's _____ keep it warm. This kind of body covering is also required in birds for _____.

The skin of a frog helps it _____ and stay

_____.

HANDS-ON Apply What You Know

Design to Survive

8. Pick an environment and describe the conditions in that environment. Then, select body parts from several animals to create a new animal that would survive there. Decide what your animal eats. Design your animal on a poster and label and describe your animal's body parts. Make sure to explain how the parts help the animal survive in its environment!

Putting It Together

9. What does an animal's external structure tell us about where it might live or eat? Suppose you encounter an animal that has a large mouth, scales, and fins. Based on this evidence about its structures, construct an argument about where the animal lives and what it eats.

_____

_____

_____

_____

Inspired by Nature

Inspirations from Nature

The animal world often provides scientists with much inspiration. Scientists and engineers study how animals use their structures to move, eat, or protect themselves and then apply what they learn to the human world. They can design useful devices that mimic, or copy, animal structures and how they function.

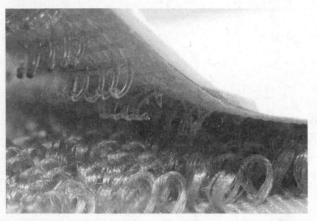

hook and loop tape

a burdock burr

Living things have structures that function to support survival, growth, behavior, and reproduction in their environments. The burrs that cling to a person's clothes serve a purpose in plant reproduction. A burdock burr is a seed that has burrs on it. The burr's function is to catch on to passing animals. The seeds will then sprout and grow when they fall in a new place.

Hook and loop tape was designed to mimic the structure of a burdock burr on fur. The function of the hook tape is to stick to the loop tape!

10. Take a look at the pictures of the different animal body coverings. Circle the letter of the animal that the burdock burr would most likely stick to.

A. snail

B. alpaca

C. tortoise

D. beetle

Same but Different

As you have learned, animals use different structures for different functions. For example, different animal coverings help in protection, insulation, or communication. Sometimes body parts with different structures in different animals have similar functions.

Comparing Animal Parts

11. Examine the pictures. Then use your observations to compare and contrast each pair of animal parts in the boxes.

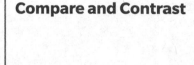
Explore Online

bat's wing

bird's wing

Compare and Contrast

eagle's beak

mountain lion's mouth

Compare and Contrast

frog's legs

dolphin's tail

Compare and Contrast

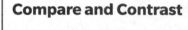

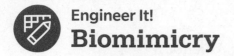

Engineer It!
Biomimicry

Scientists, engineers, and product designers may model everyday things after animal structures. This imitation of nature is called biomimetics or biomimicry.

Have you ever watched a gecko climb up a window? Gecko feet inspired the invention of Geckskin™. Most adhesives work by using something sticky, like glue, to attach things, and there is often residue left behind. Geckskin works differently. By using the full structure of a gecko's skin, scientists were able to develop an adhesive that functioned in a similar way as a gecko's feet.

▷ Explore Online

A small piece of Geckskin can hold hundreds of pounds onto a smooth surface. It works by mimicking the adhesive properties of a gecko's foot and the gecko's skin structure. This allows it to stick to a surface until it is pulled away in a certain direction.

This lizard is called a sandfish. Its body is structured to function as if it swims through sand. Scientists are trying to build robots that function in a similar way.

12. Identify two ways in which adhesives modeled after gecko feet are better than ordinary tape.

_____

_____

13. How could having a robot mimic the sandfish's movement be useful to scientists and humans?

_____

_____

 EVIDENCE NOTEBOOK Think about an animal structure that a human being could mimic. Design a model of how it could be used.

© Houghton Mifflin Harcourt • Image Credits: (l) Provided by the University of Massachusetts Amherst and Professors Al Crosby and Duncan Irschick, the inventors of Geckskin ®.. (r) ©Kristian Bell/Moment Open/Getty Images

Find the Inspiration

14. What do you think the device in the photo is? What is its function?

This device is a ornithopter. Do research to learn more about what an ornithopter is. Determine which animal structure inspired the engineering design.

Then, think of an animal that has an ability you think would be useful. Design a device that is similar in function to the ability of the animal. Then describe the function of your design and build a model of it to present to your class.

You have learned that different animals use various structures for surviving in their particular environments. Some structures may look very different but serve similar functions. For example, seal flippers and fish fins are structured differently, yet they have similar functions—swimming. Structures also may look similar but have different functions.

 Language SmArts
Summarize

15. How might studying animal structures provide people with new invention ideas?

_____

_____

_____

_____

_____

_____

_____

_____

Tip

The English Language Arts Handbook can provide help with understanding how to summarize.

Staying Warm

Skin, scales, feathers, shells, spines, and fur are different external structures of animals that help them survive.

Objective

Collaborate to investigate how an animal's covering affects its survival.

What question will you investigate to meet this objective?

_____

_____

Materials
- vegetable shortening
- spatula
- duct tape
- disposable plastic gloves
- resealable plastic baggies
- thermometer
- timer
- buckets or dish pans
- ice water, room temperature water, warm water

Procedure

STEP 1 Make a blubber mitt. Start by scooping shortening into a plastic baggie. Spread it around all the sides of the baggie, but avoid getting it on the seals.

STEP 2 Turn a second baggie inside out. Insert it into the first bag, and zip the two bags together. Use duct tape to reinforce the seal so that water cannot get inside.

What type of animal covering does this model?

_____

_____

STEP 3 Create a second mitt but without the "blubber" inside. This mitt will represent an animal's skin without a layer of fat and will be the control for the experiment.

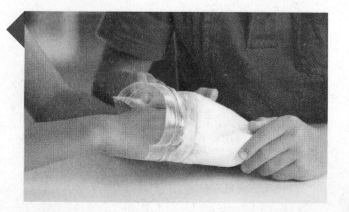

Predict how the two models will differ in the three temperatures of water you are testing.

_____

_____

STEP 4 Place one hand in each mitt. Stick both hands into the bucket of room temperature water for 1 minute. How does each hand feel? Record your observations in the table.

STEP 5 Take the temperature of the water outside the mitt with blubber, and then take the temperature inside the mitt while it is still inside the water. Record the data in the table.

STEP 6 Next, take the temperature of the water outside the mitt without blubber, and then take the temperature inside the mitt while it is still inside the water. Record your data in the table.

Temperature Inside Mitt (°F)				
Mitt	Room temp. water	Ice water	Warm water	Observations
Without shortening (control mitt)				
With shortening (blubber mitt)				

STEP 7 Repeat steps 4–6 in the warm water and then in the ice water. How did the blubber mitt feel in the ice water?

_____

_____

_____

Analyze Your Results

STEP 8 Compare the results from the blubber mitt and control mitt. Compare your results with other groups results. What did you observe about each mitt? How did they feel in the different water temperatures? Were your results similar to those of different groups? Why do you think this is the case?

_____

_____

_____

STEP 9 Describe how your blubber mitt changed in the warm water.

_____

_____

_____

Draw Conclusions

STEP 10 Which mitt provided better insulation against the cold?

_____

_____

_____

STEP 11 Polar bears have thick fur in addition to a thick layer of fat. What do you think happens to fur in water? What does this tell you about how polar bears and other Arctic animals, such as seals, survive the cold?

_____

_____

_____

_____

STEP 12 Based on your evidence, data, and model, write an argument for how an animal's covering affects its survival. What other questions would you like to ask about animal coverings?

_____

_____

_____

Discover More

Check out this path . . . or go online to choose one of these other paths.

Careers in Engineering

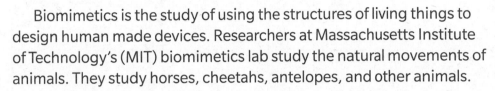

- **Balanced Parts**
- **A Feat of Feet**

Biomimetic Engineering

▶ **Explore Online**

Biomimetics is the study of using the structures of living things to design human made devices. Researchers at Massachusetts Institute of Technology's (MIT) biomimetics lab study the natural movements of animals. They study horses, cheetahs, antelopes, and other animals.

Researchers use their knowledge of biology, and may use videos, to understand how different body parts work together to produce an animal's unique walking, running, or jumping movement. Researchers then apply their understanding to design four-legged robots that move in ways similar to animals.

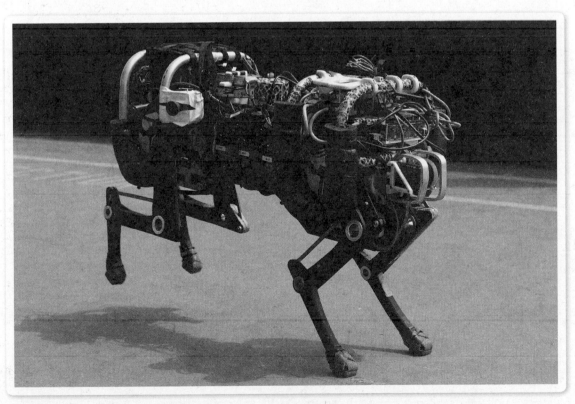

Walking may come naturally to people and animals, but it takes a great deal of coordination. It is challenging to program a robot to walk gracefully.

© Houghton Mifflin Harcourt • Image Credits: ©Mark Ralston/AFP/Getty Images

16. Suppose you are a biomimetics engineer designing a device that can help humans perform various tasks. Think about the task you would like your robot to perform. What animal movements would be helpful to mimic? How could your device be built?

Do research to learn about other biomimetic projects. Your findings should explain the evidence you found, the kind of evidence, and where you found it. Apply your findings to help you design your device. Sketch your design below. Get your teacher's approval and build a model of your device.

17. What task will your biomimetic device complete? What animal movements did you find helpful in coming up with the idea of your device? What items would you use to build your device?

_____

_____

_____

_____

_____

Lesson Check

Name _____

Can You Explain It?

Explore Online

1. Think back to the lizards from the beginning of the lesson.

   • What structures do the animals have in common?

   • How do the structures function similarly?

   • How do the structures function differently?

   • Explain how the gecko climbs vertical surfaces.

EVIDENCE NOTEBOOK Use the information you've collected in your Evidence Notebook to help you cover each point above.

_____

_____

_____

_____

_____

_____

_____

_____

Checkpoints

2. An octopus can change the color and pattern of its skin to match the environment while hunting prey. How does this help the animal?

   a. to swim

   b. to feed

   c. to play

   d. to breathe

Answer the following questions about animal structures and functions.

Choose the best answer.

3. Which of the following structures best functions to protect an animal from predators?

    a. sharp spines   **C.** colorful feathers

    b. short legs   **d.** thick fur

4. Label each animal feeding structure with what it most likely eats.

> nectar   fish   grass

_____ _____ _____

5. Draw lines to connect the structures on the left to the functions they perform on the right.

| A seagull's wings |

| A snake's fangs |

| An ant's mouthparts | | Feeding |

| A tiger's padded feet | | Movement |

| A frog's tongue |

| An ostrich's long legs |

6. Choose the best answer to complete the sentence. Biomimetics is the study of animals to

    a. help animals feed themselves.

    b. help protect animals from predators.

    c. help scientists design things to help people.

    d. help scientists change animal behavior.

302

Lesson Roundup

A. Label the structures with whether they function in *movement*, *eating*, or *covering* the animals.

_____

_____

_____

_____

_____

_____

B. Write all the correct words to complete the sentences. Some sentences may need more than one word to complete them.

> legs   fur   nature   insects   small animals

External structures for movement, include wings, fins, and

_____.

An animal's mouth shape is adapted to what it eats. A frog's large, flexible mouth and sticky tongue are suited for catching any

_____ that fit in their mouths.

In biomimetics, people design things that imitate

_____.

What Are Some Internal Structures of Animals?

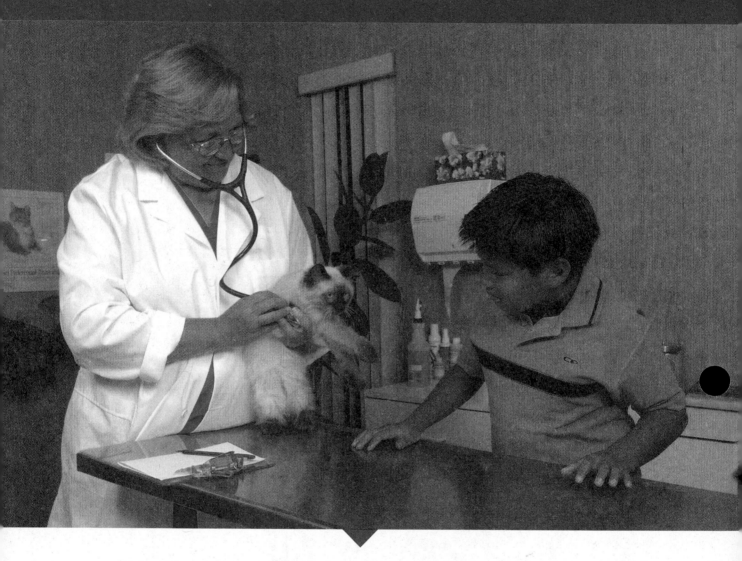

Living things have many internal structures that have specific functions. Veterinarians use a stethoscope to listen to the heartbeat of an animal.

By the end of this lesson . . .
you'll be able to provide evidence that animals have internal parts with many functions.

Can You Explain It?

a person jogging

a person sprinting

The person on the left is casually jogging while the person on the right is sprinting in a race. Think about when you jog and when you sprint. How does your body feel differently when you sprint compared to when you jog?

1. What did you observe about the runners in the photos? How do you think their internal structures are similar and different?

_____

_____

_____

_____

_____

_____

_____

_____

Tip

Learn more about how other animal structures work in What Are Some External Structures of Animals?

 EVIDENCE NOTEBOOK Look for this icon to help you gather evidence to answer the questions above.

Pumping Parts

Take a Deep Breath

When you ride your bike or do other kinds of exercise, what happens to your breathing? You might breathe faster. You might notice that you take bigger breaths, too. Take a breath right now. Think about what happens. You take air into your body. Which internal structures, or parts inside your body, fill with air? And what happens to the air after that?

Have a Heart

The respiratory and circulatory systems are how your body moves oxygen and blood around. Oxygen is a gas in air that your body needs for its basic functions. When you breathe, air enters through your mouth or nose. The air then moves along the trachea to the lungs, where oxygen moves into the bloodstream. The heart pumps this oxygen-rich blood to the body through a system of tubes called arteries. Blood is returned to the heart in tubes called veins.

2. Which is the main organ that pumps blood carrying oxygen through the body? Circle the best answer.

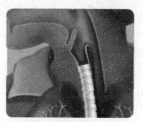
a. trachea

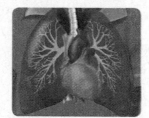
b. lungs

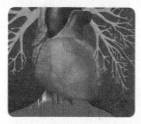
c. heart

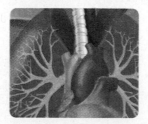
d. veins and arteries

The heart and lungs are organs. An organ is a body part that performs a function. An organ system is a group of organs that work together to do a job for the body. The lungs are the main organs of the respiratory system. The heart is the main organ of the circulatory system and is a muscular organ that can be made stronger through exercise. The respiratory system and circulatory system work together to deliver the oxygen needed in the bodies of many animals.

3. Draw lines showing the movement of air in and out of the respiratory system.

Explore Online

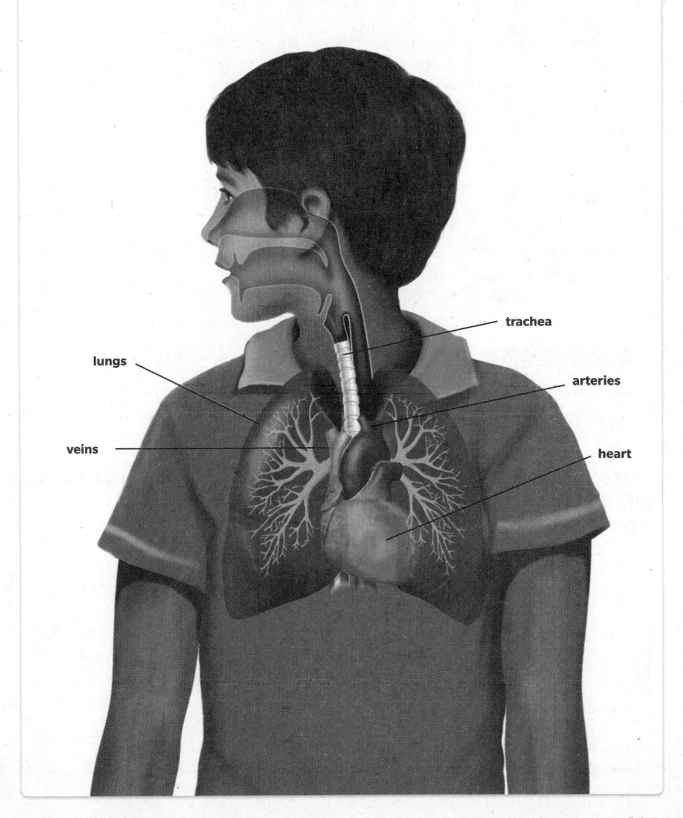

trachea

lungs

arteries

veins

heart

It Takes Teamwork!

Inhalation, or breathing in, causes air to move into the lungs. Exhalation, or breathing out, makes air leave the lungs. The diaphragm is a muscle under the lungs that controls inhalation and exhalation. When the diaphragm contracts, it moves downward. Air flows into the lungs. When the diaphragm relaxes, it moves upward, and air is pushed out of the lungs.

The heart then moves blood to the lungs, where the blood picks up oxygen. The heart then pumps the blood carrying oxygen around the body. Almost all animals need oxygen to survive. Birds, reptiles, and mammals get their oxygen from the air, and their respiratory system includes a heart and lungs. Fish use oxygen dissolved in water, and their respiratory system typically includes a heart and gills.

4. Choose the correct answer from the word bank to complete each sentence.

arteries	lungs	circulatory
respiratory	heart	lungs

In birds, reptiles, and mammals, the _____ take in air. These

organs are part of the _____ system. Oxygen is carried by blood to

the cells of the body. The blood is pumped by the _____, which is

part of the _____ system.

Do the Math
Breathing Rate

5. With a partner, count and record how many times you breathe in per minute. Take turns using the stopwatch to measure time for your partner. Record the number of breaths you take in one minute.

There are 60 minutes in one hour. Calculate and record how many times you breathe in one hour. Next, calculate and record how many liters of air pass through your lungs in an hour if each breath brings 1 liter of air into the body.

breaths per hour: _____

liters of air per hour: _____

What's the Difference?

There are similarities and differences in the internal structures of animals. Let's explore some of the ways that the circulatory and respiratory systems of animals differ.

 Explore Online

Birds and mammals have lungs and hearts with four chambers. Birds have structures called air sacs to store extra air in their respiratory systems. This makes breathing more efficient when flying.

Crocodiles have a four-chambered heart. Their systems interact in a similar way to those of birds and mammals. Other reptiles and adult amphibians have three-chambered hearts.

Most fish breathe through organs called *gills*. As water passes over the surface of the gills, oxygen is transferred to the fish's blood. Fish have a heart with two chambers.

Some invertebrates that live in water do not have respiratory or circulatory systems. In other invertebrates, air moves through a system of tubes in their bodies as they move.

 Language SmArts

Compare and Contrast

6. Which of the animals above have respiratory and circulatory systems most similar to those of humans? Describe the features that make them similar.

_____

_____

_____

Special Delivery

We do not often see the blood that is in our bodies. It is usually in the veins and arteries of the circulatory system. Although we might not see the blood in our bodies, it has many important jobs.

You've discovered that blood delivers oxygen to different parts of the body in many kinds of animals. It also carries nutrients from digested food, which the body uses to produce energy and to make and replace materials. Blood takes wastes away, too!

While blood is very important to many animals, not all animals have blood. Some invertebrates have a different but similar fluid that moves oxygen and nutrients around their bodies.

 EVIDENCE NOTEBOOK Think about the images of the runners at the beginning of this lesson. How do the circulatory and respiratory systems of these runners work together? List some problems that might happen if a person's circulatory or respiratory system isn't working well.

Putting It Together

7. Complete the table to classify the circulatory and respiratory systems of mammals, reptiles, and fish.

Compare/Contrast	Heart chambers	Respiratory system
Mammals		
Reptiles		
Fish		

HANDS-ON ACTIVITY

Pump It Up!

Objective

Collaborate to investigate the relationship between exercise and breathing rate. Your body uses oxygen for its basic functions. When you exercise, your body needs more oxygen.

Materials
- stopwatch or timer
- graph paper
- colored pencils

What question will you investigate to meet this objective?

_____

_____

_____

Procedure

STEP 1 Work in a group. Think of three kinds of exercise you could do in the classroom. Record your list. Show the list to your teacher for approval.

_____

_____

_____

STEP 2 Set the timer for 15 seconds. Count your own pulse at your wrist or at your neck for 15 seconds. Multiply this number by 4. This is your heart rate in beats per minute. Record your results in the table.

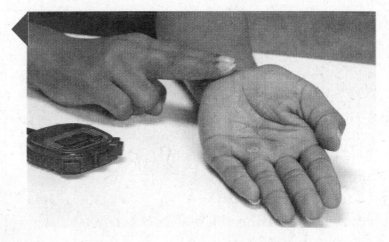

Why did you multiply the number of heart beats you counted in 15 seconds by 4?

_____

_____

_____

© Houghton Mifflin Harcourt

311

STEP 3 Do one of the exercises your group selected for one minute. After the minute is up, immediately count your pulse for 15 seconds and multiply by 4. Record your heart rate and the type of exercise you did in the table.

	Heart rate (beats per minute)			
Group member	Resting	After Exercise 1:	After Exercise 2:	After Exercise 3:

STEP 4 Repeat step 3 for the other two kinds of exercise. Make sure to wait until your pulse is back to its resting rate between exercises. Use coloring pencils and graph paper to make a bar graph.

Was your pulse rate different for different exercises? If so, why?

_____

_____

_____

_____

_____

Analyze Your Results

STEP 5 How did exercise change your heart rate or the heart rates of your group members?

_____

_____

STEP 6 Compare your results to the results of other groups. Describe any similarities or differences you notice.

_____

_____

STEP 7 This activity measured change in heart rate due to exercise. How do you think your results would be similar or different if you measured breathing rate instead of heart rate?

_____

_____

STEP 8 Usually, when a person exercises regularly, or at a higher intensity, his or her heart rate and breathing rate won't increase as much during exercise. Consider the runners in the beginning of this lesson. Which runner's heart and breathing rate probably increased the most due to exercise?

_____

_____

Draw Conclusions

STEP 9 Make a claim about exercise, breathing, and heart rate. Cite evidence from your investigation to support your claim.

_____

_____

_____

STEP 10 What other questions do you have about the effect of exercise on heart rate?

_____

_____

Food for Thought

It's Delicious!

Use the diagram on the next page to follow the path that food takes. When you take a bite of food, you might think about how delicious it is. But have you ever thought about why your body needs food? Animals need the nutrients and energy in food. They have internal parts that help them take in food and break it down.

Digestive System

Use the diagram on the next page to follow the path that food takes. Food enters the body through the mouth. Chewing helps break down the food before it's swallowed. When you swallow, food moves down a tube called the *esophagus* and into the stomach. The stomach is a muscular bag that mashes and mixes the food with substances that help break it down. By the time the food leaves the stomach, it is a liquid.

In the small intestine, chemicals made and stored by other organs, such as the liver, pancreas, and gallbladder, help break down food. The small intestine is the longest organ in the digestive system. There, nutrients from food are absorbed by the body and move into the blood. The blood distributes the nutrients to the rest of the body.

After the small intestine, the remaining material moves to the large intestine, where water and minerals are absorbed by the body. Solid waste is formed and then passes out of the body.

stomach	**small intestine**	**esophagus**
large intestine	**liver**	**gall bladder**

8. Choose the correct answer to complete each sentence.

In humans, food enters the body through the mouth and then

moves through the _____. It then moves to

the _____. In the small intestine, food is mixed

with substances produced by the _____,

_____ and the pancreas. Nutrients are absorbed by

the body in the small intestine. The remaining material moves to the

_____, where water and minerals are absorbed before

moving out of the body as waste.

Breaking It Down

9. Draw a line showing the path food takes through the digestive system.

 Explore Online

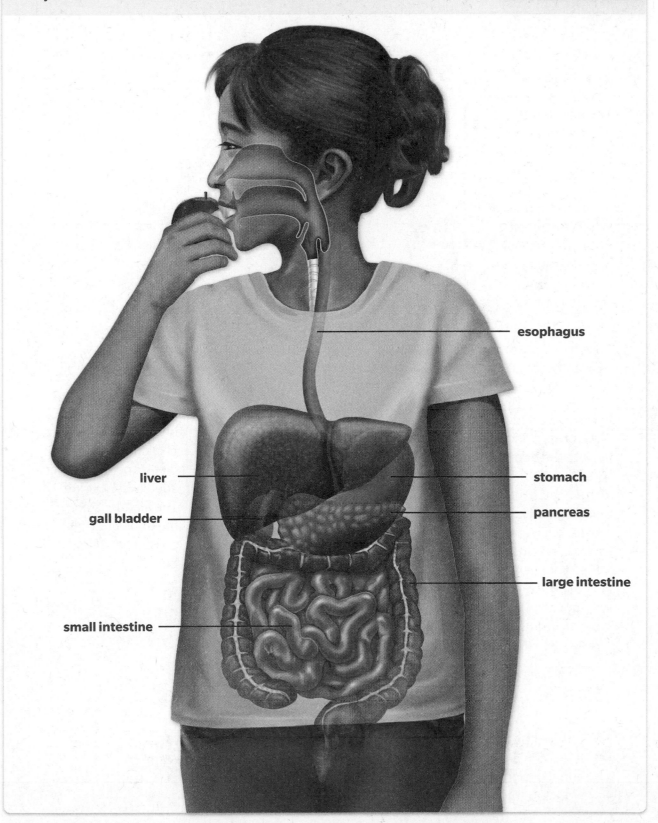

esophagus

liver

stomach

pancreas

gall bladder

large intestine

small intestine

Waste Removal

10. In school, the trash— or waste— is picked up and removed from the classroom. Your body also produces wastes that the body does not need. Draw lines from each organ to its description.

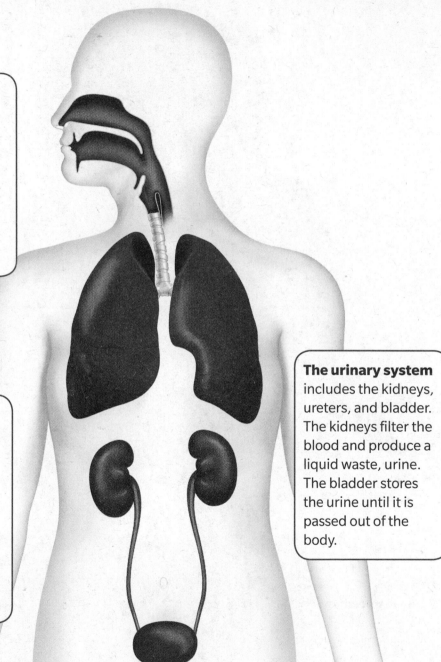

The skin is an external organ that works with internal organs to remove wastes. Sweat is produced in the skin. When you sweat, salt and chemicals are released from the body.

The lungs bring air into the body. They also help get rid of waste. The body produces a waste called *carbon dioxide*. It is a gas. When you breathe out, carbon dioxide is removed from the body by the lungs.

The urinary system includes the kidneys, ureters, and bladder. The kidneys filter the blood and produce a liquid waste, urine. The bladder stores the urine until it is passed out of the body.

 EVIDENCE NOTEBOOK In your Evidence Notebook, explain how the lungs can be part of two different body systems: the respiratory system and the excretory system. Then describe how these two body systems work together to help people grow and survive.

11. For each image, draw a star on the esophagus, a square on to the stomach, and a triangle on the intestines.

▶ Explore Online

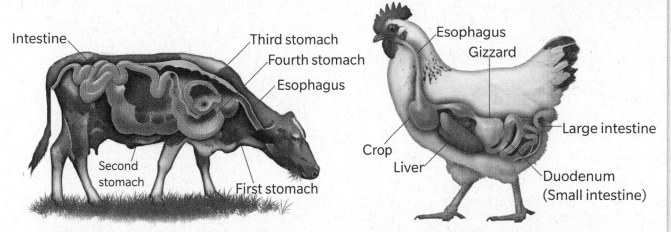

Intestine
Third stomach
Fourth stomach
Esophagus
Second stomach
First stomach

Esophagus
Gizzard
Crop
Liver
Large intestine
Duodenum (Small intestine)

Although cows and humans are both mammals, their digestive systems have big differences. Cows have stomachs with four compartments. A cow needs to chew and swallow its food several times during digestion.

Birds have an organ called a gizzard. Some birds also have an organ called a crop that holds food until it can be sent through the digestive system. The gizzard is an organ in which food is ground up by little stones the bird has swallowed.

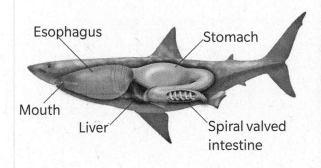

Esophagus
Stomach
Mouth
Liver
Spiral valved intestine

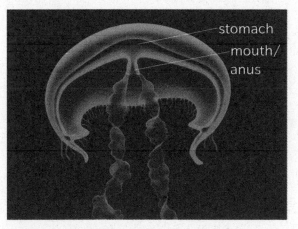

stomach
mouth/anus

A shark's digestive system needs to break down food that is often swallowed whole! Sharks have intestines shaped like a spiral and a stomach shaped like a U. This provides more surface through which the body can absorb needed materials from food.

This jellyfish is an invertebrate that does not have a digestive system. Food enters through the mouth and is broken down inside the body. There, nutrients are absorbed. Waste then leaves the jellyfish's body through its mouth.

As you can see, there are many differences among the internal structures used for digestion in animals. The functions of the digestive structures and systems are the same: to take in food, break it down to release energy and nutrients, and to absorb the nutrients and energy for use by the body.

All Systems Go

12. Choose four animals or kinds of animals. They can be the animals in the illustrations, or you can research other animals. Make a chart that compares and contrasts the digestive systems of the animals you chose. Make sure to include both similarities and differences in your chart. Submit your chart to your teacher.

13. Draw a line from the organs and body structures to the system or systems to which they belong in the human body. Some body structures may be used in more than one system.

Digestive system	lungs, kidneys, skin
Circulatory system	heart, veins, and arteries
Respiratory system	stomach, esophagus, small intestine, large intestine
Excretory system	lungs, trachea, bronchi

Language SmArts

Compare and Contrast

14. The systems in the human body have similarities. For example, the function of each system supports survival and growth. The systems have differences, too. Explain one difference between the digestive system and the excretory system.

_____

_____

_____

_____

_____

_____

Discover More

Check out this path . . . or go online to choose one of these other paths.

People in
Science

- Model Lungs
- Support Your Statements

Henry Gray and Vanessa Ruiz

Henry Gray is famous for publishing a book titled *Gray's Anatomy* in 1858. In the book, Henry Gray gave detailed written descriptions of human body structures and systems. The book also included many illustrations. The illustrations, which were drawn by Henry Vandyke Carter, showed human body systems in a detailed way. The book is still used as a medical reference today.

Explore Online

Henry Gray was an English doctor who studied anatomy.

Vanessa Ruiz is a medical illustrator and artist who combines medical illustration and contemporary art. Her images of human body structures and systems are published and shown in public spaces. She hopes to show people that medical art can be interesting. She also hopes to increase people's awareness of the structures of the human body.

Vanessa Ruiz is an artist known for her work in anatomy.

319

Animal Anatomy

15. Research the structure of different animal hearts. Find information about the structure of two-, three-, and four-chambered hearts. Then research the circulatory and respiratory systems of at least six different animals. When you have completed your research, write and illustrate a booklet titled "Anatomy of Animal Systems." Include detailed written descriptions and accurate illustrations. Be sure to list your name as author and illustrator!

Animal	Number of chambers

Lesson Check

Name _____

Can You Explain It?

1. Remember the runners? What parts inside their bodies do they use while running? How are these runners similar? How are they different? Consider:

Explore Online

- Which systems do they use while exercising?

- What happens to the body during exercise?

- How does frequent exercise change people's body systems?

📝 **EVIDENCE NOTEBOOK** Use the information you've collected in your Evidence Notebook to help you cover each point above.

_____
_____
_____
_____
_____
_____
_____
_____

Checkpoints

2. What would be the result of a person getting a disease that affected the lungs?
   a. blood would not be pumped through the body
   b. it would be hard to breathe.
   c. food would not be broken down
   d. wastes would not be filtered from the blood

3. Which of the following aid in breaking down food? Circle all that apply.
   a. stomach
   b. heart
   c. lungs
   d. small intestine

4. What is the function of this structure? Circle the best answer.
   a. to carry food from the mouth to the stomach
   b. to release the nutrients in food
   c. to release substances needed to break down food
   d. to allow nutrients from food to move into blood

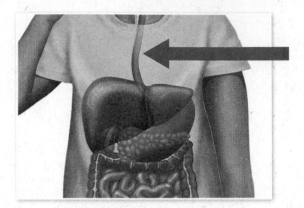

5. Draw a line from the system to the function it performs.

digestive system	bringing in oxygen
circulatory system	breaking down food
respiratory system	removing wastes
excretory system	moving materials through the body

6. Which statements correctly describe these organs? Circle all that apply
   a. part of the respiratory system
   b. found in all animals
   c. part of the excretory system
   d. take in oxygen

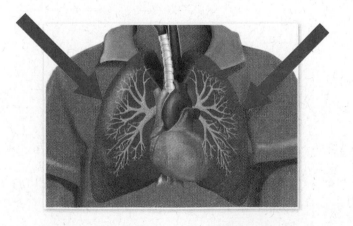

Lesson Roundup

A. Draw a line from the type of heart to the organism it belongs to.

four-chambered heart	fishes
three-chambered heart	mammals, birds
two-chambered heart	amphibians

B. Choose the correct answer for each sentence.

excretory	**respiratory**	**circulatory**	**digestive**
kidney	**stomach**	**gizzard**	**air sac**

In mammals, the _____ system breaks down food.

Organs that are part of this system include the _____ and

the small intestine. The _____ system removes wastes from

the body. Other kinds of animals have different structures as parts of these

systems. For example, birds have a _____ in which food is

broken down.

C. Draw a line from the organ to the system it belongs to. Some organs
may belong to more than one system.

lungs	digestive system
stomach	circulatory system
skin	respiratory system
heart	excretory system

How Do Senses Work?

A peacock mantis shrimp has very complex eyes. Humans have three kinds of receptors to detect light. A peacock mantis shrimp has twelve! It uses its eyesight and other senses and traits to improve its chances of survival.

By the end of this lesson . . .
you'll be able to construct an argument that animals have internal structures to support survival and behavior.

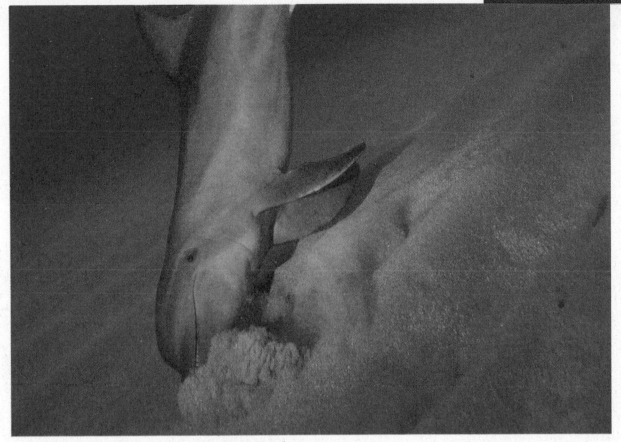

Animals use their senses to obtain and process information about their environment. Dolphins often swim and search for food in dark or murky water where they cannot see using their eyesight.

1. How do you think dolphins find food in dark water, especially if what they are looking for does not make any noise? What other sense might they use to "see" without using their eyesight?

_____

_____

_____

_____

Tip

Learn more about parts animals use to move about in their environments in What Are Some External Structures of Animals?

 EVIDENCE NOTEBOOK Look for this icon to help you gather evidence to answer the questions above.

Touchy, Feely

Body Senses

Have you ever touched something hot with your hand? How did you react? You probably responded by pulling your hand back very quickly!

The Skeletal and Nervous Systems

2. Look at the image showing systems in your body that work together, then match the description to the part it describes.

Explore Online

a. Humans and many other animals have a **skeletal system** mainly made of bones. The skeletal system gives structure, support, and protection to the softer parts of the body.

b. The nervous system contains some very important parts of the body—the **brain**, the spinal cord, and the nerves. The brain is the central processing organ and is protected by the skeletal system.

c. The nervous system contains two kinds of **nerves**: those that send information to the brain or spinal cord, and those that send information from the brain and spinal cord to the rest of the body.

d. The **spinal cord** is a bundle of special nerve fibers and tissue that connects almost all the parts of the body to the brain. It is protected by the backbone. The brain and the spinal cord make up the central nervous system.

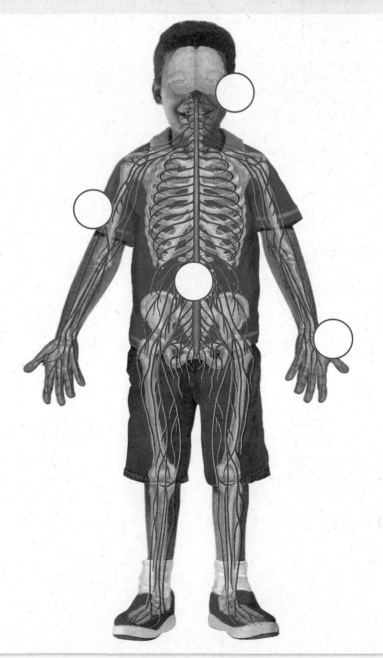

Skin Deep

The largest organ in your body is your skin. It provides protection by covering your entire body. Skin also contains special structures called **receptors**. Receptors respond to changes inside and outside the body and report them to your nervous system. These changes may form perceptions and memories that could guide your actions.

There are three main types of skin receptors: touch, temperature, and pain. All three nerve endings can receive different kinds of information that comes to the skin from the environment.

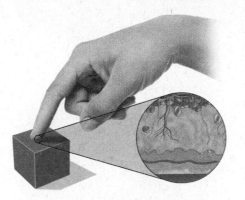

Touch and pressure receptors react to how hard, soft, rough, or smooth an object is. When you touch something like a wood block, receptors send nerve signals to your brain. The brain processes these signals so that you know what you are holding.

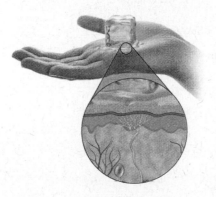

If you are holding an ice cube, you quickly realize that your hand is freezing! This is because temperature receptors in your skin react to the temperature of the ice cube and send nerve signals to the brain.

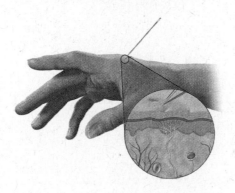

When the skin feels intense pressure or is injured, pain receptors send information about the pain to the central nervous system. The central nervous system processes the signals and causes the muscles to try to move away from the source of the pain. The body's reaction to pain is immediate.

Humans aren't the only organisms, which are living things, that have a central nervous system for controlling the body. All mammals, fish, insects, and birds rely on a central nervous system. Simpler animals have a more basic kind of nervous system.

Feel It

Test your understanding of how skin works by answering each of the questions below.

3. A friend places a warm rock in your hand. Which types of information about the rock will your skin receptors most likely receive? Circle all that apply.

   a. color

   b. taste

   c. weight

   d. temperature

4. In most cases, where does the information sent from skin receptors in your hand get processed?

   a. in the brain

   b. in the hand

   c. in pain receptors

   d. in the tips of the fingers

5. Which kind of receptor do you think would relay the message to your brain if you were cut? Circle your answer.

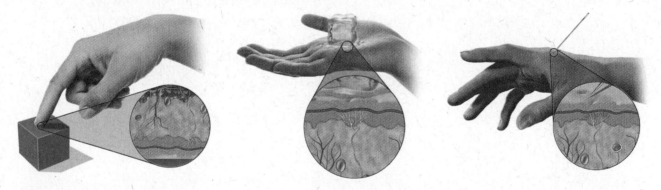

Language SmArts
Identifying Main Ideas and Details

6. How do your senses react to things in your environment?

_____

_____

_____

_____

Knee-Jerk Response

Not all sensory information travels to the brain to be processed. Has your doctor ever checked your reflexes?

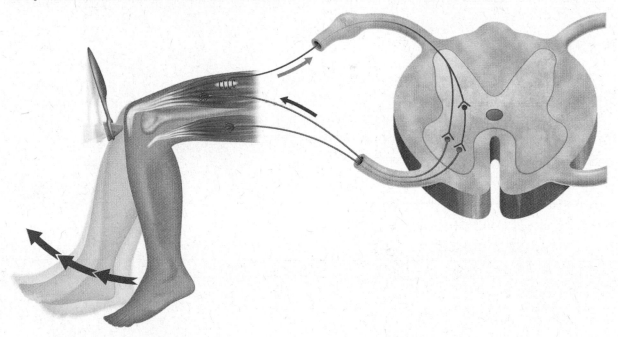

Certain body parts have receptors that send information to the spinal cord. From the spinal cord, a response is immediately sent back to the muscles. The brain is not involved. These reactions are called reflexes. Reflexes are important to the survival of many animals because they allow animals to respond more quickly to their environment.

 EVIDENCE NOTEBOOK Think about how dolphins might use their sense of touch to catch food.

Putting It Together

Show what you've learned about the different kinds of sensory receptors.

7. Compare and contrast touch receptors, temperature receptors, and pain receptors.

_____

_____

_____

_____

_____

HANDS-ON ACTIVITY
Touch Test

Objective

Collaborate to investigate how receptors work in your body. The sensory receptors in your skin are not arranged evenly across your body. Some parts of your body may have more of one kind of receptor but fewer of another. Find out which parts of your body are more sensitive to touch and pressure.

Materials
- 2 paper clips bent into a V-shape
- metric ruler
- pencil or pen

What question will you ask to meet this objective?

_____

_____

_____

Procedure

STEP 1 Open and bend the paper clip into a V-shape so that its ends are about 2 cm apart. Use a metric ruler to measure the distance. Make sure the two halves of the V-shape are the same length.

STEP 2 Ask your partner to rest his or her hand, palm side down, on a flat surface. Tell your partner to look away.

STEP 3 Lightly press both ends of the paper clip into the back of your partner's hand. Do not press too hard! Make sure both ends touch the skin at the same times.

Why do you not want to press down too hard with the paper clip?

_____

_____

_____

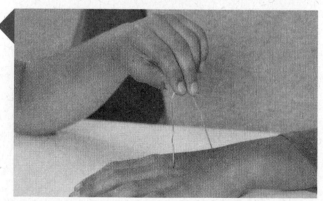

© Houghton Mifflin Harcourt

STEP 4 Ask your partner if he or she felt one or two pressure points. If your partner feels one point, spread the ends of the paper clip apart and test again. If your partner feels two points, push the ends a little closer together and try again. When your partner FIRST feels two points, record the distance between the paper clip's ends.

Think back to Step 1, in which you were instructed to make sure both halves of the V-shaped clip were the same length. Why was that important?

_____

_____

STEP 5 Repeat steps 2 and 3 three more times. Record your results in the second column of the data table by writing the smallest distance at which your partner reported feeling two points.

STEP 6 Repeat steps 2–5 on the right calf, the right shoulder, and the inside of the right forearm. You can use another data table and repeat steps 2–4 with your partner doing the testing using a new paper clip.

	Distance		
	Trial 1	Trial 2	Trial 3
Hand			
Shoulder			
Calf			
Forearm			

Analyze Your Results

STEP 7 What was the shortest distance record on your data table? What was the greatest distance?

_____

STEP 8 On what part of the body were two points of the paper clip felt at the shortest distance?

_____

STEP 9 On what part of the body were two points felt at the greatest distance?

_____

STEP 10 On what part of the body did it take the most tries to feel two distinct points of the paper clip?

_____

_____

Draw Conclusions

STEP 11 How did your results compare to your partner's results?

_____

_____

_____

STEP 12 Based on your results, which of the four parts of the body tested is the most sensitive on your partner? On you?

_____

_____

STEP 13 Compare results with other groups in the classroom. How are they similar? How are they different?

_____

_____

_____

STEP 14 Make a claim about senses. Support your claim with evidence from your observations in this activity.

_____

_____

_____

STEP 15 Think of other questions you would like to ask about senses.

_____

_____

_____

Is That Something I Want to Eat?

How the Nose Knows

▷ Explore Online

You've learned about the receptors in your skin. But did you know that you also have receptors in your nose?

Every time you breathe air into your nose, receptors inside the nose sense different chemicals in the air. These smell receptors are attached to nerves that send signals to the brain about those chemicals. This is how you are able to smell odors and aromas in the air.

You probably think you have a strong sense of smell. But compared to other mammals, a human's sense of smell isn't very good. Mice have the second strongest sense of smell of all mammals.

8. Write the word that best completes each sentence.

You are able to smell odors and aromas because you have smell receptors in

your _____. Elephants have the strongest sense of smell. The

trunk of the elephant contains touch and _____ receptors.

🖐 **HANDS-ON Apply What You Know**

Name That Scent!

Try a simple activity to test your sense of smell. Blindfold your partner and see how many smells he or she can identify correctly. Hold a scented item in front of your partner's nose. Keep track of your results. Switch with your partner and repeat.

9. Did your results surprise you? Why or why not? Which scents did you guess correctly?

_____

_____

_____

_____

_____

Need Salt?

Like your skin, your tongue has receptors to receive information from its environment: the mouth and whatever you may be drinking or chewing. The tongue has receptors that allow you to taste and feel what you eat and drink.

Which Receptor?

10. Explore how the sensory receptors of your tongue work. Then match the adjectives to the receptor they describe.

Explore Online

Taste isn't the only characteristic of food that's important. Touch receptors on your tongue let you know about the texture of what you eat and drink. Some things are smooth, some things are lumpy, and some things are rough.

It's also important to know the temperature of your food. When the temperature receptors of your tongue come into contact with what you are eating or drinking, they send signals to your brain letting you know how hot or cold it is.

The taste buds are the receptors on your tongue that sense salty, sweet, bitter, sour, and umami (savory) flavors. Every time you take a bite of something, taste buds send signals to the brain to let you know how your food tastes.

Occasionally, you might eat or drink something that's too hot, too spicy, too cold, or too sharp. The pain receptors on your tongue let your brain know when you're better off letting food cool off, warm up, or be avoided completely.

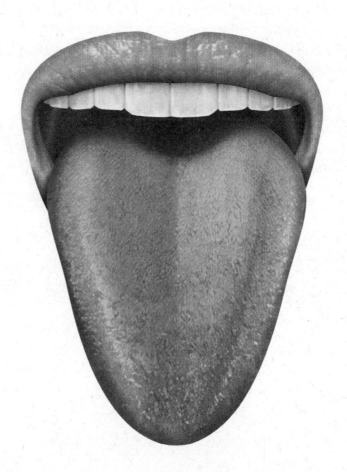

sour	smooth
sweet	cold
boiling	spicy
grainy	warm

Taste	Touch	Temperature	Pain

No See, No Smell, No Taste?

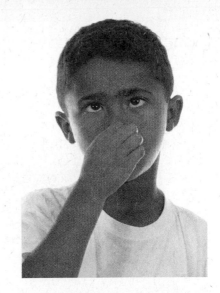

Your nose is more important than you might think, especially when it comes to tasting foods.

Surprisingly, much of your ability to taste comes from your smell receptors. Even though your taste buds react to salty, sour, sweet, savory, and bitter flavors, it's your smell receptors that allow you to specifically identify a particular food.

Blindfold a partner, then give him or her four different foods to eat. Have your partner hold his or her nose. Ask him or her to identify the food. Switch with your partner and repeat using four different foods.

11. What are your results? How do you think your daily life would change if you could not smell?

_____

_____

_____

12. Discuss the results with your partner. Talk with your classmates about the ways we use smell in our daily lives.

 EVIDENCE NOTEBOOK Dolphins are mammals, just like us. However, they don't have a sense of smell. Why do you think the sense of smell wouldn't be useful to dolphins? Record your ideas in your notebook.

 Language SmArts
Cause and Effect

13. Is there a food you avoid because of the way it smells or tastes? How might an animal in the wild benefit from a strong smell or taste response?

_____

_____

Tip

The English Language Arts Handbook can provide help with understanding how to make cause and effect connections.

Sights and Sounds

Eye See!

Along with the skin, tongue, and nose, there are also sensory receptors in the eyes. Many animals have specialized receptors that receive different types of information through the eyes.

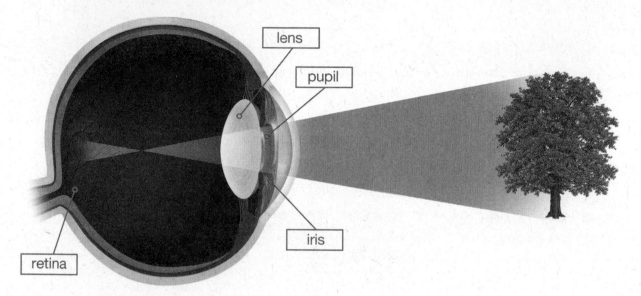

Light bounces off an object. It then enters the eye through an opening at the center of the iris called the *pupil*. The iris is the part of the eye that has color. After passing through the pupil, light strikes the back of the eye. At the back of the eye is an area called the *retina* where there are light receptors. These receptors react to the light and send nerve signals along a pathway to the brain, where the information is processed.

But How Does It See?

14. Circle the structures that allow each animal to "see."

Pigeons see color just like humans. But they can also see ultraviolet light, unlike humans.

Dogs and cats can see with their eyes, but they rely more on scent and sound for their survival than on vision.

Some snakes see in two ways. They see color and have vision pits in their faces that allow them to *see* heat.

Here's to the Ears!

There are sounds everywhere, but you wouldn't be able to hear any of them without the hearing receptors in your ears. As you have learned, senses allow humans and other animals to receive different kinds of information. This information is carried by nerves to the brain. The brain processes the information, causing the body to react and respond to the information in different ways.

Animals have different levels of sensitivity to sound. Many animals are able to produce and hear lower or higher sounds than humans can hear.

All Ears

15. Explore the image that shows the parts of the ear and their functions. Match the caption to the part of the ear it describes.

 Explore Online

a. The *outer ear* is the part of the ear you can see. The shape of the outer ear funnels sound into the ear, through the ear canal, and toward the middle ear.

b. The ear drum separates the outer ear from the *middle ear*. The middle ear is an air-filled area with three small bones: the hammer, the anvil, and the stirrup.

c. The *inner ear* contains the fluid-filled cochlea and the semicircular canals. The sound vibrations from the middle ear cause the fluid, and the thousands of tiny hairs inside the cochlea, to move.

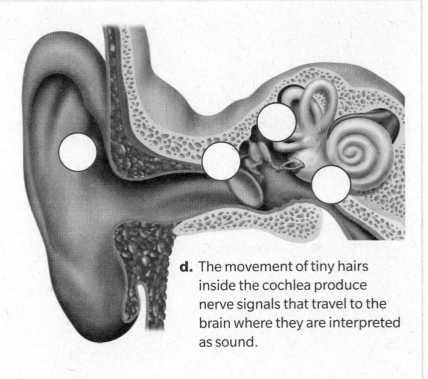

d. The movement of tiny hairs inside the cochlea produce nerve signals that travel to the brain where they are interpreted as sound.

Language SmArts
Opinion

16. How do you feel when you hear music? To answer, associate words that describe your memories of music and sound with words that describe feelings.

_____

_____

"Seeing" By Hearing

Bats are the only flying mammals. As they fly at night, bats send out sounds through their mouth and nose. When the sounds hit an object, the sounds bounce back, or echo, and are funneled into the bat's ears. As in humans, the sound vibrations move through the ear and are converted to signals sent along nerves to the brain. There the information is processed. Bats use echolocation to locate food, navigate while flying, and find their way home.

17. How do you think bats use echolocation to tell the difference between small objects and large objects?

_____

_____

_____

_____

HANDS-ON Apply What You Know

Test It!

18. Blindfold your partner. Make clicking noises in front of, to the left of, to the right of, and behind your blindfolded partner. Observe how your partner uses the clicking noises to locate your position.

  EVIDENCE NOTEBOOK How do you think dolphins might use sound to find their prey in murky water? Record your ideas in your notebook.

Putting It Together

Think about what you've learned about how animals see, hear, and smell.

19. Why is it important for their survival that animals see, hear, and smell in different ways?

_____

_____

_____

_____

Discover More

Check out this path . . . or go online to choose one of these other paths.

Extreme Senses

- Eye Check
- What Colors Do You See?

Extreme Senses

The greater wax moth is one of the favorite food sources of bats. Fortunately for the moth, it is often able to escape being eaten by using its extreme sense of hearing.

Greater wax moths can hear sounds in the same range as the bats who are trying to catch them. The moths then move in a way that makes it difficult for the bats to find them. This makes it much easier for the moths to avoid being eaten and survive.

Mantis shrimp are about four inches long but they are one of the strongest animals in the world. They use clubs to punch their prey at very high speeds. This incredible force is important for hunting food and to protect itself and its home.

The mantis shrimp is not a mantis, nor is it a shrimp. It is more closely related to lobsters and crabs. It has special structures in its eyes that scientists believe allow it to see and process information quickly.

Moth

Mantis shrimp

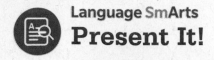

Language SmArts
Present It!

20. Research 5–10 other living things that have extraordinary senses. Find out how these senses are used for survival. Present your findings to the class in a multimedia presentation and submit your presentation to your teacher. Use the chart below to record your notes for your presentation.

Extreme Creatures	
Organism	**Extreme senses**

21. What did you learn about extreme senses? Which was your favorite? If you could have an extreme sense, what would it be?

_____

_____

_____

_____

_____

_____

Lesson Check

Name _____

Can You Explain It?

1. Think back to how bats use their senses to receive and process information about their environment. How is the dolphin's environment like that of a bat's? How do you think a dolphin uses its senses to "see" its surroundings without using its eyes? Be sure to do the following:

   • Discuss the internal structures the dolphin might use.

   • Describe the receptors that might be involved.

   • Step through the whole process the dolphin uses, ending with it eating a fish.

Explore Online

> **EVIDENCE NOTEBOOK** Use the information you've collected in your Evidence Notebook to help answer these questions.

_____

_____

_____

_____

_____

_____

_____

Checkpoints

2. Suppose you mistakenly rest your hand on a hot stovetop. What are some ways your nervous system will respond? Select all answers that are correct.
   a. Your brain will tell your arm muscles to pull the hand away.
   b. Your nervous system will wait for your muscles to respond.
   c. Your brain will remember that stovetops can be hot.
   d. Your pain receptors will send messages to the brain.

3. Match each situation to the kind of receptor that reacts.

seeing a green lizard running	pain receptor
sweet piece of fruit	sight receptor
hand is poked by a sharp object	taste receptor

4. Use the image to help you choose the correct answer for each sentence.

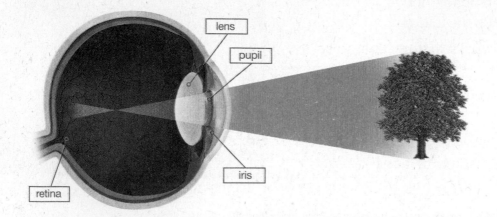

The eyes contain _____ receptors that react to light. Light passes

through the _____ of the eye to reach the receptors.

5. What do you predict will happen if you hold your nose while eating your lunch? Circle the best answer.
   a. My lunch won't taste as good.
   b. I'll eat my lunch more quickly.
   c. My taste buds won't be able to function.
   d. The food in my lunch won't look the same.

6. How do sounds get from the inner ear to the brain? Circle all that apply.
   a. They pass through the eardrum.
   b. They make tiny hairs move in the cochlea.
   c. They are translated by receptors into nerve signals.
   d. They cause fluid to move in the outer and middle ear.

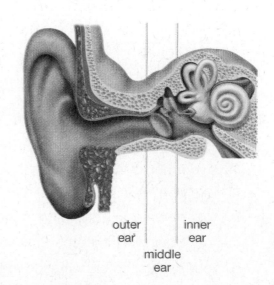

outer ear   inner ear

middle ear

Lesson Roundup

A. Choose the correct words that complete each sentence.

> **skeletal system**   **nervous system**
>
> **brain and spinal cord**   **central nervous system**

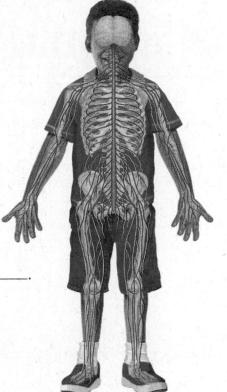

The _____ includes the brain,

spinal cord, and all the nerves in the body. The central

nervous system includes just the _____.

Sensory receptors are constantly reacting to things

inside and outside the body. The reactions are sent to the

_____ as nerve signals.

....

B. Choose the correct words that complete each sentence.

> **taste   sight   smell   hearing   touch**

You use your sense of _____ to choose your favorite

meal. A cheetah uses its sense of _____ to spot the

weakest zebra in a herd. A bat uses its sense of _____ to

fly at night, searching for food. A hungry grizzly bear uses its sense of

_____ to find the most fragrant berries to eat.

....

C. Choose the sense that reacts to each example. Place the example in the correct column.

> **red   bumpy   spicy pepper   scent of pencil shavings**
>
> **smooth   pin dropping   lion roar   sour cherry**

Touch	Taste	Smell	See	Hear

ENGINEER IT!

Breathing In and Out

You work for a medical company that manufactures a product for those with asthma and other breathing difficulties. The portable invention is designed to fill its user's lungs with fresh air. The company has decided to develop a version of this product for young people. Your team is tasked with gathering data on the lung capacity of fourth-grade students.

How much air can this fourth-grader's lungs force into this balloon?

DEFINE YOUR TASK: What kind of data is it your goal to uncover?

_____

_____

Before beginning, review the checklist at the end of this Unit Performance Task. Keep those items in mind as you proceed.

RESEARCH: Use online or library resources to learn about ways of measuring human lung capacity. If necessary, divide your research into two separate areas—ways to capture air from lungs and ways to measure that air. Examine multiple sources, and cite the ones you use.

_____

_____

_____

_____

BRAINSTORM/ASSEMBLE DATA: As a team, come up with at least two methods of safely gathering air from human lungs. Then discuss ways of accurately measuring that air once it is gathered.

_____

_____

_____

PLAN YOUR PROCEDURE: Consider the questions below as you plan your data-gathering procedure.

1. What materials, tools, and equipment will you need?
2. How will you gather air from your test subjects' lungs?
3. How will you measure the quantity of the air you gather?
4. How many test subjects will you use?
5. How will you record, graph, and present your results?
6. Will you express your final data as a single number or as a range? Why?

_____

_____

_____

_____

PERFORM AND RECORD: Get your teacher's approval. Then, perform your procedure as you planned it. Examine your data, and summarize your results.

_____

_____

COMMUNICATE: Tell the class about your research, your procedures, and how you arrived at the data you were looking for. Display any graphs or charts that can help you communicate your results.

☑ Checklist

Review your project and check off each completed item.

_____ Includes a description of the data being sought.

_____ Includes a list of cited sources.

_____ Includes options considered for gathering and measuring air from lungs.

_____ Includes a thorough description of the test procedure, including materials used.

_____ Includes results expressed as written or charted data.

_____ Includes an oral presentation on your procedures, results, and conclusions.

Unit Review

1. An inventor develops an adhesive based on the substance a gecko uses to hold itself to glass. What term best describes how a design can imitate things found in nature? Circle the correct choice.

   a. biostructures

   b. adaptations

   c. camouflage

   d. biomimicry

2. Which of the following qualities demonstrates how a frog's skin is adapted to its environment? Circle all that apply.

   a. It is thin.

   b. It is slimy.

   c. It is warm.

   d. It is moist.

3. Use the word bank to complete the sentences.

   | animals   nectar   plants |

   The flat teeth of antelope are teeth suited to eating _____ .

   The sharp teeth and jaws of alligators are suited to eating _____ .

4. Classify each structure as helpful for protection (P) or motion (M):

   _____ Fur

   _____ Fins

   _____ Legs

   _____ Wings

   _____ Shells

   _____ Spines

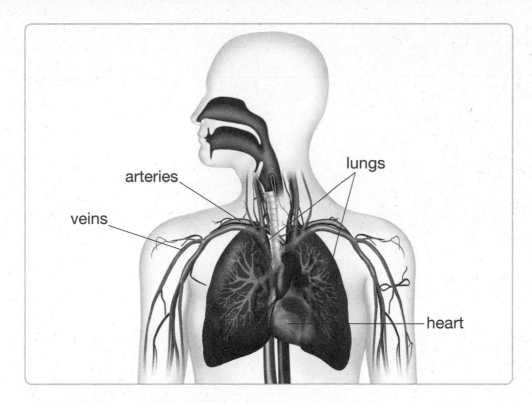

arteries

veins

lungs

heart

5. Use the word bank to complete the sentences.

| oxygen | circulatory | respiratory | excretory |

This drawing shows the _____ and _____

organ systems. These two systems work together to move _____

and other gases through the body.

6. Why is the circulatory system considered a *system*? Explain the parts that work together and the function of those parts.

_____

_____

_____

_____

7. Which of these are part of the human excretory system? Circle all that apply.

a. skin

b. lungs

c. heart

d. kidneys

8. Which sense does this animal sometimes use to "see" in murky water? Circle the correct choice.

    a. taste

    b. touch

    c. smell

    d. hearing

9. Sophia plays basketball at her elementary school. She uses her brain, eyes, and nerves to play the sport. Explain how these three parts of her body work together to manage her movements when she's trying to catch the ball.

_____

_____

_____

_____

_____

10. Use the word bank to complete the sentence.

touch	smell	temperature
sight	pain	taste

There are three general types of receptors in human skin:

_____ , _____ , and _____ .

Interactive Glossary

As you learn about each item, add notes, drawings, or sentences in the extra space. This will help you remember what the terms mean. Here is an example:

fungi (FUHN•jee) A group of organisms that get nutrients by decomposing other organisms

hongos Un grupo de organismos que obtienen sus nutrientes al descomponer otros organismos.

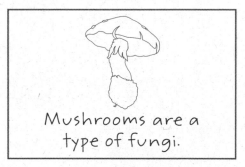

Mushrooms are a type of fungi.

Glossary Pronunciation Key

With every glossary term, there is also a phonetic respelling. A phonetic respelling writes the word the way it sounds, which can help you pronounce new or unfamiliar words. Use this key to help you understand the respellings.

Sound	As in	Phonetic Respelling	Sound	As In	Phonetic Respelling
a	bat	(BAT)	oh	over	(OH•ver)
ah	lock	(LAHK)	oo	pool	(POOL)
air	rare	(RAIR)	ow	out	(OWT)
ar	argue	(AR•gyoo)	oy	foil	(FOYL)
aw	law	(LAW)	s	cell	(SEL)
ay	face	(FAYS)		sit	(SIT)
ch	chapel	(CHAP•uhl)	sh	sheep	(SHEEP)
e	test	(TEST)	th	that	(THAT)
	metric	(MEH•trik)		thin	(THIN)
ee	eat	(EET)	u	pull	(PUL)
	feet	(FEET)	uh	medal	(MED•uhl)
	ski	(SKEE)		talent	(TAL•uhnt)
er	paper	(PAY•per)		pencil	(PEN•suhl)
	fern	(FERN)		onion	(UHN•yuhn)
eye	idea	(eye•DEE•uh)		playful	(PLAY•fuhl)
i	bit	(BIT)		dull	(DUHL)
ing	going	(GOH•ing)	y	yes	(YES)
k	card	(KARD)		ripe	(RYP)
	kite	(KYT)	z	bags	(BAGZ)
ngk	bank	(BANGK)	zh	treasure	(TREZH•er)

A

amplitude (AM•pluh•tood) A measure of the amount of energy in a wave. p. 156

amplitud Medida de la cantidad de energía en una onda.

aquatic fossil (uh•KWAH•tik FAHS•uhl) The remains or traces of an organism that lived in water long ago. p. 492

fósil acuático Restos o vestigios de un organismo que vivió en el agua hace mucho tiempo.

C

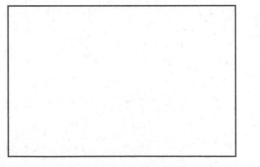

collision [kuh•LI•shuhn] The result of two objects bumping into each other. p. 128

colisión Resultado del choque entre dos objetos.

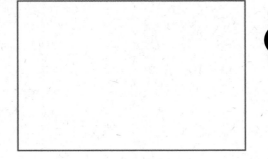

constraint (kuhn•STRAYNT) Something that limits what you are trying to do. p. 9

restricción Algo que limita lo que se está tratando de hacer.

continent (KON•tn•uhnt) One of the seven largest land areas on Earth. p. 409

continente Una de las siete áreas terrestres más grandes de la Tierra.

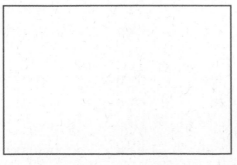

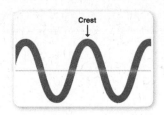

crest (KREST) The top part of a wave. p. 156

cresta Parte superior de una onda.

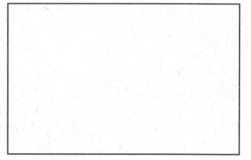

criteria (kry•TEER•ee•uh) The desirable features of a solution. p. 8

criterios Características deseables de una solución.

D

deposition (dep•uh•ZISH•uhn) The dropping or settling of eroded materials. p. 359

deposición Caída o asentamiento de materiales erosionados.

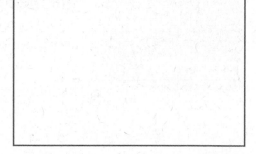

desert (DEZ•ert) An area of land that is very dry. p. 380

desierto Superficie de tierra muy seca.

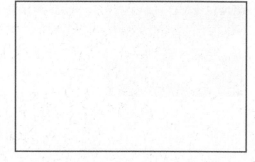

D

design process (dih•ZYN PRAHS•es) A series of steps that engineers can follow to make solutions that meet a need or want.

proceso de diseño Serie de pasos que los ingenieros pueden seguir para desarrollar soluciones que cumplan con un requisito o una necesidad.

drawback (DRAW•bak) A disadvantage or problem. p. 538

inconveniente Desventaja o problema.

E

electric current (ee•LEK•trik KER•uhnt) The flow of electric charges along a path. p . 72

corriente eléctrica Flujo de cargas eléctricas a lo largo de una trayectoria.

elevation (el•uh•VEY•shuhn) The height of the land above sea level. p. 416

elevación Altura de la tierra sobre el nivel del mar.

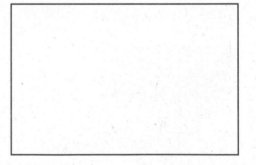

energy (EN•er•jee) The ability to do work and cause changes in matter. p. 70

energía Capacidad de realizar una tarea y causar cambios en la materia.

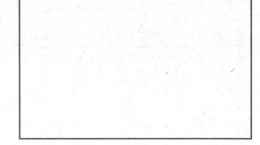

energy transfer (EN•er•jee TRANZ•fuhr) The movement of energy from place to place or from one object to another. p. 78

transferencia de energía Movimiento de energía de un lugar a otro o de un objeto a otro.

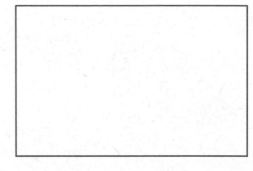

energy transformation (EN•er•jee TRANZ•fuhr•may•shuhn) A change in energy from one form to another. p. 78

transformación de la energía Cambio en la energía, de una forma a otra.

engineering (en•juh•NIR•ing) The use of scientific and mathematical principles to develop something practical. p. 6

ingeniería Uso de principios científicos y matemáticos para desarrollar algo práctico.

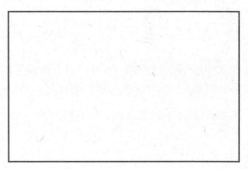

E

erosion (uh•ROH•zhuhn) The process of moving sediment from one place to another. p. 359

erosión Proceso de mover el sedimento de un lugar a otro.

external structures (EX•tuhr•nuhl STRUK•churs) Those parts on the outside of a body or structure. p. 286

estructuras externas Partes que se encuentran fuera de un cuerpo o estructura.

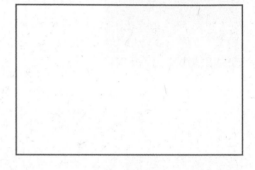

extinct (ex•STINGT) Describes a kind of thing that is no longer found on Earth. p. 484

extinto Describe cierto tipo de ser vivo que ya no se encuentra en la Tierra.

F

failure analysis (fail•UR uh•nal•UH•sis) Figuring out what went wrong and why. p. 50

Análisis de falla Averiguar lo que salió mal y por qué.

fair test (FARE test) A test that does not give any advantage to the conditions or objects being tested. p. 33

prueba justa Una prueba de que no cualquier ventaja de las condiciones u objetos están probados.

fertilization (fur•tl• uh•ZEY• shuhn) The process when male and female reproductive parts join together. p. 257

fertilización Proceso en el que se unen los órganos reproductivos del macho y la hembra.

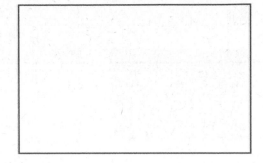

fossil (FAHS•uhl) The remains or traces of an organism that lived long ago. p. 484

fósil Restos o vestigios de un organismo que vivió hace tiempo.

H

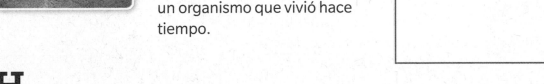

heat (HEET) The energy that moves between objects of different temperatures. p. 90

calor Energía que se mueve entre objetos con temperaturas distintas.

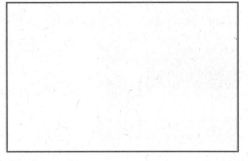

I

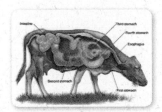

internal structures (IN•tuhr•nuhl STRUK•churs) Those parts on the inside of a body or structure. p. 306

estructuras internas Partes que se encuentran dentro de un cuerpo o estructura.

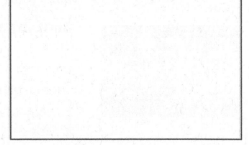

L

leaf (LEEF) The part of a plant that makes food, using air, light, and water. p. 235

hoja Parte de la planta que es capaz de generar alimento usando aire, luz y agua.

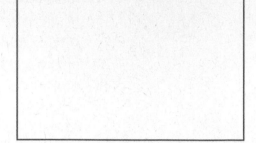

N

natural hazard (NACH•er•uhl HAZ•urd) An earth process that threatens to harm people and property. p. 574

peligro natural Proceso terrestre que amenaza con dañar a personas y bienes.

natural resource (NACH•er•uhl REE•sawrs) Materials found in nature that people and other living things use. p. 528

recurso natural Materiales que se encuentran en la naturaleza y que las personas y otros seres vivos utilizan.

nonrenewable resource (nahn•rih•NOO•uh•buhl REE•sawrs) A resource that, once used, cannot be replaced in a reasonable amount of time. p. 529

recurso no renovable Recurso que, después de haber sido utilizado, no podrá ser reemplazado en un tiempo razonable.

O

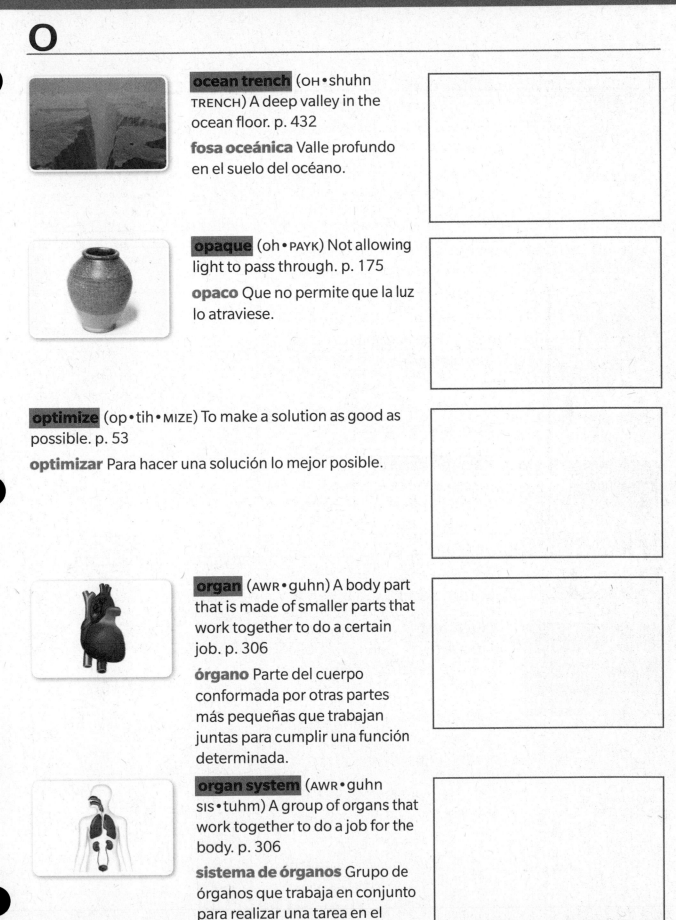

ocean trench (OH•shuhn TRENCH) A deep valley in the ocean floor. p. 432

fosa oceánica Valle profundo en el suelo del océano.

opaque (oh•PAYK) Not allowing light to pass through. p. 175

opaco Que no permite que la luz lo atraviese.

optimize (op•tih•MIZE) To make a solution as good as possible. p. 53

optimizar Para hacer una solución lo mejor posible.

organ (AWR•guhn) A body part that is made of smaller parts that work together to do a certain job. p. 306

órgano Parte del cuerpo conformada por otras partes más pequeñas que trabajan juntas para cumplir una función determinada.

organ system (AWR•guhn SIS•tuhm) A group of organs that work together to do a job for the body. p. 306

sistema de órganos Grupo de órganos que trabaja en conjunto para realizar una tarea en el cuerpo.

P

pollination
(pol•uh•NAY•shuhn) The
transfer of pollen in flowers or
cones. p. 257

polinización Transferencia del
polen en flores o conos.

pollution (puh•LOO•shuhn)
Waste products that damage an
ecosystem. p. 536

contaminación Todo
desperdicio que daña un
ecosistema.

prototype (PROH•tuh•typ) A working model used for
testing a solution.

prototipo Modelo de trabajo que se utiliza para probar
una solución.

R

rain forest (RAYN FOR•est)
A dense forest found in regions
with high heat and heavy rainfall.
p. 380

bosque lluvioso Bosque denso
que se encuentra en regiones
de altas temperaturas y fuertes
lluvias.

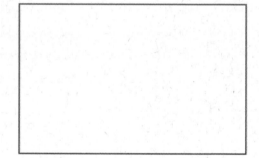

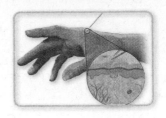

receptors (ree•SEP•turs) Special structures that send information about the environment from different parts of the body to the brain. p. 327

receptores Células nerviosas especiales que envían información acerca del ambiente desde la piel hasta el cerebro.

reflection (rih•FLEHK•shuhn) The bouncing of light waves when they encounter an obstacle. p. 176

reflejo Rebote de las ondas de luz cuando encuentran un obstáculo.

relative age (REL•uh•tiv AYJ) The age of one thing compared to another. p. 461

edad relativa Edad de una cosa al compararla con otra.

renewable resource (rih•NOO•uh•buhl ree•SAWRS) A resource that can be replaced within a reasonable amount of time. p. 550

recurso renovable Recurso que puede ser reemplazado en un tiempo razonable.

reproduction (ree•pruh•DUHK•shuhn) To have young, or more living things of the same kind. p. 257

reproducción Tener cría o generar más seres vivos del mismo tipo.

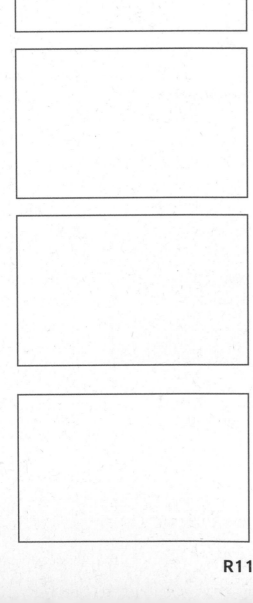

R

resource (ree•SAWRS) Any material that can be used to satisfy a need. p. 528

recurso Cualquier material que pueda ser utilizado para satisfacer una necesidad.

root (ROOT) A plant part that is usually underground and absorbs water and minerals from the soil. p. 235

raíz Parte de la planta que usualmente es subterránea y que absorbe agua y minerales del suelo.

S

scale (SKEYL) The part of a map that compares a distance on the map to a distance in the real world. p. 412

escala Parte de un mapa que compara la distancia en el mapa con la distancia en el mundo real.

seed (SEED) The part of a plant that contains a new plant. p. 262

semilla Parte de la planta que contiene una nueva planta.

spore (SPOR) A reproductive structure of some plants, such as mosses and ferns, that can form a new plant. pp. 235, 263

espora Estructura reproductiva de algunas plantas, como los musgos y los helechos, que puede generar una nueva planta.

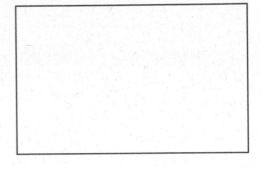

stem (STEM) The part of a plant that holds it up and has tubes that carry water, minerals, and nutrients through the plant. p. 235

tallo Parte de la planta que la sostiene y que tiene conductos que llevan agua, minerales y nutrientes a través de toda la planta.

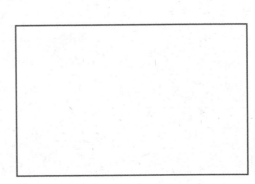

T

terrestrial fossil (tuh•RES•tree•uhl FAHS•uhl) The remains or traces of an organism that lived on land long ago. p. 492

fósil terrestre Restos o vestigios de un organismo que vivió en la tierra hace mucho tiempo.

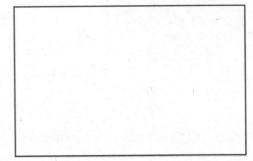

translucent (trahns•LOO•suhnt) Letting some light through. p. 175

translúcido Que deja pasar parte de la luz.

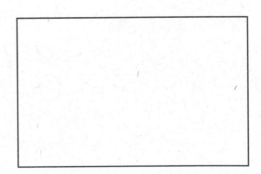

T

transparent
(trahns•PAIR•uhnt) Letting all light through. p. 175

transparente Que deja pasar toda la luz.

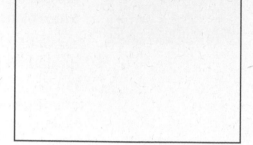

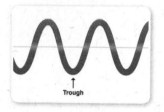

trough (TROF) The bottom part of a wave. p. 156

depresión Parte inferior de una onda.

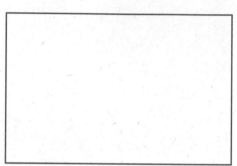

V

vibrate (VY•brayt) To move back and forth. p. 102

vibrar Moverse hacia delante y hacia atrás.

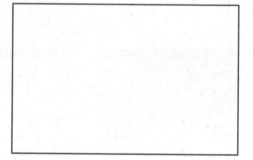

volume (VAHL•yoom) How loud or soft a sound is. p. 158

volumen Cuán alto o bajo es un sonido.

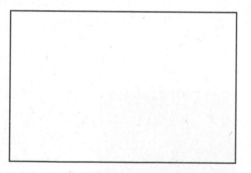

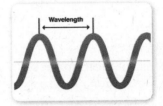

wave (WAYV) The up-and-down movement of surface water. It can also be a disturbance that carries energy through space. p. 149

ola Movimiento hacia arriba y hacia abajo de la superficie del agua.

onda Alteración que lleva energía por el espacio.

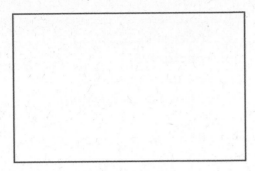

wavelength (WAYV•length) The distance between a point on one wave and the identical point on the next wave. p. 156

longitud de onda Distancia entre un punto en una onda y ese mismo punto en la próxima onda.

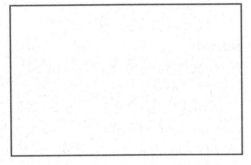

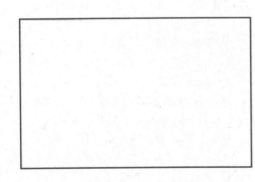

weathering (WETH•er•ing) The breaking down of rocks on Earth's surface into smaller pieces. p. 359

desgaste Descomposición de las piedras de la superficie terrestre en piezas más pequeñas.

© Houghton Mifflin Harcourt • Image Credits: (b) ©iStockphoto.com

Index

A

acoustic engineers, 38–39
aerial photo, 406
air pollution, 73, 540–542
Akaroa Head (New Zealand), 459
algae farming, 73
Alps, 459
Alvarez, Luis and Walter, 514
amber, 493
amplitude, 156–158, 162–163
Anderson, Clayton, 249
anechoic chamber, 34, 36–37
animals
   adaptations to environment, 381
   alpaca, 290
   ammonite, 492, 495
   antelope, 289
   ants, 287, 493
   archerfish, 186
   Bactrian camel, 381
   bat, 287, 338, 339
   beaver, 384
   birds, 290, 309, 317
   body coverings, 286, 290–292, 296–298
   cat, 336
   circulatory system, 306, 308–310
   clam, 493
   corals, 493, 495
   cow, 317
   crocodile, 309
   crustaceans, 505
   digestive system, 314–318
   dog, 336
   dolphin, 287, 325
   dragonfly, 493
   eagle, 289
   elephant, 219–220, 333
   fish, 186, 309, 492, 495–496, 505
   frog, 287, 289
   gecko, 285, 294
   greater wax moth, 339
   Irish elk, 488
   jellyfish, 317
   lizards, 285, 294
   meerkat, 382
   mosasaur, 489
   mosquito, 289
   mountain lion, 289
   mouse, 333
   mouth parts, 289, 293
   peacock mantis shrimp, 324, 339
   pigeon, 287, 336
   plesiosaur, 484
   polyp, 495
   respiratory system, 306–309
   sambar deer, 381
   sandfish, 294
   sea cucumber, 290
   shark, 287, 317
   snail, 492
   snakes, 152, 290, 336, 505
   sounds of, 155, 219–220
   structures for movement, 287–288, 293, 295
   termite, 384
   tubeworm, 289
   turtles and tortoises, 290, 501
anther, 256
anvil (ear), 337
aquadynamic testing, 35
arch, rock, 475
argument, 50, 267, 291, 298
artery, 306, 310
Artiles, Mayra, 83

B

Badlands of South Dakota, 464–465
bark (tree), 235, 237
base isolator, 581
batteries, 74, 78–79, 82–83, 567–568
beach erosion, 151, 358, 369, 396
beak, 293
beats (tuning), 164
binary code, 210–211, 214–215
binoculars, 189
biomass fuel, 73, 550
biomimicry (biomimetics), 292, 294–295, 299–300
Birling Gap, England, 358
bits (in binary code), 210, 212–213
bladder, 316
Block, Adrienne, 442
blood, 306–310
brain, 190–191, 326, 337
brainstorm, 601
breathing, 306–307, 308, 311–313
bridge (rock formation), 475
British Thermal Unit (Btu), 532
Buckley Formation (Antarctica), 459
buffering, electronic, 212–213
buoy, 150–151, 606
burr, 292
burrow, 382

C

cable, telegraph, 204–205
camera lens, 188
canyon formation, 462, 471–472, 475
carbon dioxide, 90, 316

© Houghton Mifflin Harcourt

© Houghton Mifflin Harcourt